SECRETS OF A STRESS FREE RETIREMENT...

"How To Make Sure You Don't Outlive Your Nest Egg!"

written by Benjamin Greenhill

SECRETS OF A STRESS FREE RETIREMENT...

"How To Make Sure You Don't Outlive Your Nest Egg!"

Foreword

BY BOB EUBANKS, 3 TIME EMMY AWARD WINNING HOST OF THE NEWLYWED GAME.

 Hi, I'm Bob Eubanks. If you're like me as you've gotten older, you probably have had concerns about the years to come. You may be worrying whether or not you will have enough money to last during your retirement years. What if tragedy strikes and you or your spouse need to stay at a long term care facility? How will you afford it? Or worse yet, how would you survive, financially speaking, if your spouse died?

These are just a few of the many obstacles you may face having the potential to wipe out your nest egg. However, with a little planning and better understanding of the rules of the game, your retirement years could be golden.

While reading this book, you will be shocked to realize that there are many financial pitfalls that exist in the world of retirement today. Some snafus are government imposed while others may come from negligence or mistakes from trusted advisors. But regardless, this book shines the light on some of the dangers that lurk in the dark, giving you the tools and knowledge to make the proper plans to protect yourself and your family. It is written in plain English so you don't have to be a lawyer to understand it. The stories throughout this book leave you with a clear understanding of what can go wrong and how you can avoid some of these mistakes.

In 1964, I borrowed $25,000 on my house in order to bring The Beatles to the Hollywood Bowl Concert (their first West Coast Performance). Back then that was a HUGE amount of money. But, that was an investment that really paid off for me. It was the beginning of a 20-year concert promotion career that included The Beatles, The Rolling Stones, Barry Manilow, Elton John and Bob Dylan, just to name a few. Plus, I even have to attribute landing the position as host of the Newlywed Game to this bold beginning.

In those days, taking big risks was scary, however, I knew even if I lost everything and had to start over... I still had my youth. But as we get older and wiser, we tend to be more worried about money and our health.

As you read this book you will have a better idea of where you are financially. And, if you are not where you want to be, you will discover many options to help get you there. So, grab yourself a cup of coffee and find a cozy spot to start your journey.

Sincerely,
Bob Eubanks

CONTENTS

Chapter 1

PEOPLE DON'T PLAN TO FAIL, THEY SIMPLY FAIL TO PLAN

ഓ

Sometimes old clichés get a little worn, and people feel they're trite and insignificant. However, the other side of the coin is to understand why they became clichés in the first place. People use them over and over because there is simply a lot of truth to them.

As we said (a cliché, if you will):

People don't plan to fail, they simply fail to plan.

What's the truth that lies in this cliché? Let me give you an example and see if any of this sounds familiar.

Bert and Charlene wanted to see if we could help them plan for their retirement.

Now the fact that they had both recently turned 65 and wanted to start planning for their retirement might sound a little odd to you. In fact, it's just the opposite. People like Bert and Charlene come in all the time wanting to plan for their retirement...at the exact time they are retiring.

They had met in high school, been married for 42 years, raised three children, and had seven grandchildren. They had known each other their entire adult lives. Now they finally reached the point of retirement age and they wanted to be sure they were okay, financially speaking.

Let me ask you a question.

Do you really think it's a good idea to start planning for your retirement exactly when you turn age 65 and are ready to retire?

Bert and Charlene didn't plan too much for their retirement before they retired. They just kind of assumed everything would work out. They had managed to get by financially their whole lives by having things sort of "work out."

They figured out how to get two kids through college (their youngest daughter never went to college but did require financial help with her baby when her husband left her) and they'd always managed to take care of financial emergencies like dental braces, broken furnaces, a new roof, etc.

So there they were. Charlene retiring from her job as an assistant to the superintendent of a school district, and Bert, who owned a pharmacy in town and had sold it to his cousin. They just sort of assumed everything would work out fine. Between the two of them, they had over $412,000 saved up in retirement plans. Their home was almost paid-for, and they had very few other debts. For Bert and Charlene, having $412,000 in one place at one time seemed like a heck of a lot of money. Now that they had retired they decided to come into our office to do retirement planning.

(As we go through the book, we'll tell you all about how to plan for your retirement and go into much more detail about how to analyze your financial situation and help you figure out what to do based on case studies like Bert and Charlene's.)

When Bert and Charlene were presented their plan, they became upset. Very upset. Why? Well, because when the plan showed them that based on their goals, how much money they wanted to have, and the things they wanted to do, their retirement nest egg wouldn't last them more than 9-10 years.

Somewhere around age 75, they would be basically broke and living on Social Security and Charlene's small pension. They were very angry and wanted to know how anyone could tell them such a stupid thing.

Anyone would know that $412,000 was a ton of money. They worked their whole lives to save up all this money, and it should be able to last them through retirement. And who were we to tell them they couldn't make it?

We are not being critical in any way of Bert and Charlene. But, Bert and Charlene made a very big mistake. They made the assumption they could start planning their retirement the day they retired.

That's much like planning your wedding on the day of your wedding. Most people are familiar with the concept of planning for a wedding, and no one in their right mind would consider getting up on Saturday morning, making some phone calls and hoping everything went well that afternoon.

Bert and Charlene made a classic mistake.

They didn't plan to fail, they simply failed to plan.

It's been our experience that Americans procrastinate more about financial decisions than about other things they need to deal with.

We will generally be very diligent about planning for all sorts of things in our lives, but when it comes to money, we just simply don't do it. We find all sorts of reasons why we can't:

2

"We'll start planning when the kids are older..." "We'll start planning when I get my new job...." "We'll start planning when we get back from vacation ..." "We'll start planning when the house is finished…" "We'll start planning when the kids are done with school ..." "We'll start planning once the car is fixed..." "We'll start planning when I get my degree..." "We'll start planning once..." All these reasons, excuses, and rationalizations. And, the bottom line is planning for your financial future is probably one of the most important things you can do with your time.

As you read through this book and listen to the stories and case studies and think about your own life, please understand there is one thing we want you to get out of this book if nothing else:

You have to plan for your financial future, because nobody is going to take care of you... but YOU!

The government won't take care of you,
and your company won't take care of you.

The only person who will take care of you...is YOU!

Chapter 2

THE LOST SECRET OF PLANNING

&

If you look in the dictionary, the word "planning" is defined as: "To form a scheme, a method for doing, achieving, etc." Something we do for virtually everything we accomplish in our lives. Everything except for our financial future, that is.

When you think about it, it just makes so much sense to take the time to plan for your future.

There are three steps you need to plan for the future that we will cover in this book.

1. First, finding out where you are today,
2. Second, where you want to go, and,
3. Third, building a plan to get there.

It's that simple and that complicated.

To start out, review and think about the following commonly asked questions:

1) What is my net worth?
2) Where are my assets?
3) Why do I own these assets?
4) How are they titled?
5) How much will these assets earn before I retire?
6) If I'm already retired, what should I do with these assets?
7) How much do I need for food, clothing, shelter, travel and other non-investment expenses?
8) Where does the money come from to pay for these expenses? (Savings, income, social security, etc.?)
9) How much will these expenses cost tomorrow?
10) How much will they cost ten years from now?
11) Will my current income keep up with inflation and the cost of living?
12) What tax bracket am I in?
13) What income tax planning has to be done to minimize taxes in my tax bracket?
14) What would I want to happen if I got sick, mentally incapacitated or died in the near future?
15) What have I done in regards to estate tax planning?
16) Do I have any unrealized capital gains that may have to be paid someday?
17) What taxes do I need to consider when investing?

Good questions, don't you think? Can you honestly say you can answer them?

Let me give you an example of how planning works and how important it is to help you make informed, educated decisions.

John and Mary Smith are both 57 years of age. They have no children living at home, and they are currently in the 25% tax bracket. They have $100,000 ($130,000 originally) left on their mortgage. Their monthly principal and interest payments are approximately $779 based on a 6% mortgage rate. They currently have $150,000 in CDs earning 3%, which represents most of their investments.

Would John and Mary be better off paying off some or all of the mortgage today?

This is a common question, and most Americans don't really know how to figure out which makes the most sense for them. Although every family has a different situation, let's look at some of the facts in this case so that we can help John and Mary make an informed decision.

John and Mary have always been told that paying off their mortgage early was a bad idea because they get a tax deduction on the interest. However, the critical question most people forget to look at is, "At what point does the interest deduction continue to make sense?"

Let's look at some simple facts: The Smith's make around $4,500 per year in earnings on their CDs. After paying 25% income taxes, they end up with only about $3,375. In addition, they currently pay $9,348 in yearly mortgage payments. Out of that amount, approximately $7,200 is deductible interest. At a 25% tax bracket this means that the Smiths can save $1,800 (25% of $7,200) in taxes.

The real calculation is done by comparing the after-tax rates of return on both of the options, and then deciding. The CDs earn 3%, but after paying taxes at 25%, they really only earn 2.25%. Therefore, the Smith's investments are growing by 2.25%. Their 6% mortgage rate is really 4.5% after taking into account that the interest rate of 6% is tax deductible.

So, they are making 2.25% after taxes on the CDs, and losing 4.5% after-taxes on the mortgage! They are losing 2% every year! (2.25% CD net return less 4.5% mortgage cost = -2%.) Since they are paying more than they are making, it would make sense that they increase their net worth by using the CD money to pay off the home.

In essence, investing in the home and paying the mortgage off would actually be more profitable!

This can be quite confusing because even though they saved money in taxes, they had actually lost money! This is because they paid more in interest than they made.

5

On the other hand, if the Smith's had been in other investments instead of the CDs and were making 9%, the numbers would look different. Now their 9% taxable return would produce 6.75% in after tax return, which is higher than the 4.5% after tax cost of the mortgage, providing actual growth because they're earning more after tax...than the cost of the loan after tax!

So, in this example, they'd be better off not paying off the mortgage because they are earning more than the after tax cost of the loan.

If this is confusing, don't worry, most people find tax rules confusing. The important thing to remember is that with knowledge and some good advice the average American could save thousands of dollars each year with proper planning.

Your financial situation will always have a major impact on your family and your family's well being. It's very hard to separate our lives from our money.

As we move through this book, let's keep in mind how important this issue of planning is. You will see everything we talk about, everything we teach, everything we counsel people on is centered on planning, planning, and more planning.

It is truly the lost secret of the ages. Once you understand where you are, where you want to go and what options and choices you have on how to get there, you can make better decisions. Decisions based on a complete understanding of the options that you have acquired through planning.

You'll be in the best possible position. You'll be making choices based on an understanding of the options, the pros and cons, and know that you're working in a logical and scientific manner... as opposed to just doing things based on emotion, salespeople's pressure, your brother-in-law's sage wisdom or something you heard on CNN.

No one can guarantee success. No one can guarantee you won't have financial problems. No one can guarantee things will go perfectly. It would also be ridiculous for us to make those statements.

What we **can** do and say with confidence is:

Planning will give you the best chance to reach your goals!

Planning will give you the best chance to deal with problems and changes in your life and in the economy. Planning will provide you the best chance to achieve the peace of mind and contentment we all are seeking.

Sometimes we feel we are a lone voice in the wilderness crying out saying, "Please people, plan your future, plan your finances, take the time to do it!"

Many financial advisors are more than happy to sell you products based on what they want you to buy, and/or sell you products based on the commissions they earn.

Some firms talk about financial planning, but very few really take the time to figure out what your situation is, and how to help you make the best objective choices based on the best options available for you to reach your goals.

We're going to teach you more about that in this book.

Our focus has always been based on planning and we hope that yours is, too.

Think about it. Planning is defined as:

"to form a scheme, a method for doing, achieving, etc."

There are three steps to plan for the future:

1) **Find out where you are today.**
2) **Decide where you want to go.**
3) **Build a plan to get there.**

If you leave this book with a better understanding of how things really work, and how to think correctly about planning for your own future and well-being, you will be well on your way to a peaceful retirement!

Chapter 3

SIX WAYS TO LOSE OR
RUN OUT OF YOUR MONEY

ℰↃ

No retiree ever wants to run out of money. No retiree ever wants to lose his money. No retiree ever wants to be dependent. Unfortunately, all of these things happen far too often.

Most retirees haven't been advised, or learned how, to set up a financial plan that will allow them to protect themselves from any of the six major ways one can lose or run out of money. Most folks aren't aware of these until they experience them.

These six areas continue to cause problems for retirees. Problems that can be reduced or eliminated through proper planning. As we go through this book, we will be discussing these various areas in much more detail, and how you can protect yourself from them through knowledge and planning.

For now, we want to introduce these six dangerous items, have a brief discussion about them, and set the stage for later chapters in the book where we will discuss them in more detail.

In our opinion, the six dangers causing the most problems for retirees, and creating the greatest chances for them to lose or run out of money are:

1. Taxes.
2. Catastrophic medical expenses.
3. Inflation.
4. Bad investment planning.
5. Lawsuits.
6. Passing away without having a proper estate plan.

Any one, or a combination of these items, can wipe out an entire life's savings, sometimes overnight! We're not trying to scare you here. In fact, just the opposite. This book is based on reality, and sometimes reality isn't pleasant.

Many retirees learn far too late about any one, or all of these six items. It's our job in this book to help you be aware of them, and know how to deal with them, so that there is as little chance as possible that they will affect your financial security.

We don't want you saying, "How could this happen to me?

So we want to give you the tools, knowledge and questions to ask so you can avoid having to say that altogether.

Now, let's briefly discuss the six items and how they can affect you and your retirement security.

1. Taxes

You would think it would go without saying that retirees would want to pay as little tax as possible. That retirees would want to use every legal advantages available to them to reduce their taxes. But that's not the case.

Most retirees that we see who haven't done planning are paying more taxes than necessary. They're paying maximum income taxes. Most retirees have their situations set up so that they don't take advantage of more than a few, if any, of the tax savings advantages that are available to them.

We'll go into more details about tax savings opportunities in Chapter 5, but for now we want to make sure you understand you are not required to pay the most amount of taxes possible. It's your right, and, in fact, one judge said it's your duty to learn about all the advantages available to you under the law and take maximum advantage of them to reduce your taxes!

Think about this.

If you saved $200 a month in income taxes by rearranging your financial affairs, and invested that money at only 4%, over a period of 10 years, it would grow to a sum of over $25,000!

That's $25,000 of money that you would otherwise have squandered if you'd paid it in taxes, because once it's gone, it's gone. Wouldn't you rather keep that money? Saving $200 a month in taxes is child's play for most retirees if, and this is the big IF, they take the time to learn about the strategies they can take advantage of to save them money.

Keep in mind that every year there are usually hundreds of changes made to the IRS rules! They've recently changed all kinds of laws on things like capital gains, estate taxes and so on. If you don't know how to integrate these changes into your plans, you could easily make mistakes that could cost you hundreds or even thousands of dollars.

We think it is an absolute shame to see so many retirees sending their hard earned money off to Washington on a one-way trip to never be seen again. Don't let taxes ruin your financial security. Make sure you keep this in mind when you read Chapter 5, and pay attention to the legal advantages and strategies we're going to show you for saving taxes.

2. Catastrophic Medical Expenses

The health care crisis in America is real and out of control. The government has been a major contributor to this crisis, and does not know what to do about it. But the fact that it's a mess doesn't change your situation. It doesn't help you to say it's a mess and blame the problems on the government and insurance companies. You need to take care of your own situation.

43% of the people reading this book are going to spend some time in a nursing home, according to the U.S. government. That's 43%. Almost half. (Source: New England Journal of Medicine.) In fact, with increased survival to age 65, the number of 65 years olds ultimately using nursing homes are projected to double by 2020.

You have got to plan how you're going to take care of your long term health care needs since the odds are very high that at some point you will either have to stay in a nursing home, or require long-term care.

Sure, your health insurance and Medicare will pick up most medical expenses while you're in the hospital, but they won't pick up the bulk of the costs of long-term care once you leave. In fact, Medicare pays nothing for long-term care other than a limited amount for the first 100 days, and then only a small percentage of the people who apply for it actually receive it.

We'll discuss catastrophic medical expenses in more detail in Chapter 10. We want you to start thinking about the fact that the way the program is set up now, you are responsible for long-term care expenses, and other uninsured medical expenses not covered by Medicare or your health insurance.

Just remember, nearly half of the people reading this book will spend some time in a nursing home or require long-term care, which is currently running $7,000 a month on average (this is projected to be between $9,000 - 12,000 a month within 10 years).

The laws are always changing! It's very important to get the proper legal and financial advice before implementing your retirement plan!

Extended care, whether at home or in a nursing home, is unfortunately a fact of life that needs to be addressed today. In order to protect yourself and your loved ones from the catastrophic effects of outrageous medical expenses, it is wise to obtain the services of an expert. Don't make the common mistake of thinking that you can interpret the ever-changing laws yourself.

You either have to have a plan to change the way your assets are owned, get the proper insurance to cover this sort of expense, or take the risk of being wiped out. This is not a pleasant topic, but it must be faced and addressed head on.

Long-term medical care is the Achilles heel in most retirement plans. Yet it need not be if addressed early on. There are many new and creative plans available today that were not on the market a few years ago.

3. Inflation

We'll go into much more detail about inflation in Chapter 4, but we just wanted to briefly mention that inflation in and of itself has destroyed more retirements than any other factor we've ever seen.

As we just mentioned, about half the people reading this book may have to spend time in a nursing home. That's bad. What's worse is that inflation affects all of the people reading this book. Inflation is defined as the "cost of things you have to buy going up in price." Inflation is not going away, is not under control, and can devastate your financial situation.

Even though the government tries to downplay the role of inflation, from our point of view, we cannot downplay it at all. We've seen too many people outlive their money, be forced to reduce their standard of living significantly, and depend on friends, family and charity to survive, simply because inflation took what was once a comfortable fixed income at one point in their life...and turned it into a meager, if not unlivable, income as the years rolled by.

Don't think for a second that just because the government says inflation is licked, that it really is. The rate of inflation fluctuates. And while the statistics issued by the government say the inflation rate is under control, it is not okay.

For example, the government statistics say that inflation is running around 3% as of the writing of this book. But, when you look at how prices have escalated on so many items that directly affect you, there's no way that a 3% figure is realistic for the average American.

Just look at what gas prices have done in the past couple years..."It's Crazy!"

Prices go up constantly, and retirees must face the fact that they must plan their retirement future with inflation as part of that plan in order to have a realistic chance of realizing their goals without altering their life-style, dramatically changing how they live, and/or facing the very real prospect of literally out-living their money.

So, yes, inflation is a very real danger that will affect everyone, and one you don't have the option to ignore.

4. Bad Investment Planning

This is another big problem area where we see retirees continuing to make mistakes. Mistakes and problems that often cause them great distress during their retirement.

Many people don't understand what investments are, or how they work. Most people are not even sure if a CD is an investment. It can be very complicated and confusing.

Our purpose in this book is not to give you detailed, technical explanations of different investments. What we are trying to do is point out that if you plan for the future and you have investment planning integrated with your other financial planning, you will know what kind of returns you need to achieve to make your plan work. You'll learn what options you have available to you though the planning process so you can make educated decisions, diversify your portfolio, and have a truly solid investment plan that will give you the best chance of reaching your goals!

Of course, you need to establish goals first. Then you need to understand what rate of return you need to earn to make your plan have the best chance of working, and then how you have to diversify to make those earnings possible. That can only come through planning.

Unfortunately, most people buy investments out of greed, and sell out of fear.

They buy investments because they want them to increase in value and expect that they will. If the investment drops in value, they sell out of fear sometimes at prices far below what they paid. This causes destruction of their net worth and their portfolios.

Similarly, many people like to "wait" to see how high a mutual fund will go before they buy it. This kind of thinking makes no sense. Tell us one other asset that you would buy where you wait until it goes up higher and higher in price before you bought it. If you buy a car, don't you want to buy it at the lowest cost? Not the highest. Or, do you wait to see if the price increases, and then decide to buy it?

The stock market is the only market in the world where when the price goes down, everyone "runs out of the store!"

Investments only work if you buy low and sell high!

Your portfolio must be diversified, and set up to meet your goals while considering the risk that you are willing to assume. We will cover those risks in more detail along with more issues about investing in Chapter 13 (Investment Choices Made Easy: The Right Choices).

12

For now, we want to plant the seed that your retirement will be greatly affected by how your investments are set up and perform. Investing improperly, buying high/selling low, or making investment decisions for the wrong reasons will cause many sleepless nights, and there's no need for that.

5. Lawsuits

Most retirees don't realize that lawsuits are a common plague, and can cost them some or all of their life savings. Many retirees wonder why they would be sued. They might wonder, "I'm not in business anymore? I'm not in the work force?," and so on. The answer is very simple.

There are lots of ways you can get sued. Many of them are ridiculous and unfair, but, nevertheless, a fact of life.

Believe us, if you back out of your driveway and accidentally run over a child on a bicycle, you will be sued. If you spill coffee on your neighbor's lap, you could be sued. If you invest in your son's business and become a board member, you could be sued. If you are out in the world in any way today, you can be sued.

You must set up your assets properly. Know how your things should be owned and how the titles on assets should be set up. And be sure that your liability insurance is set up properly.

One brief instant, one blink of an eye, one incident, can cause you to lose your entire net worth and everything you have saved.

6. Passing Away Without Having Properly Set Your Estate

This is another area where we see families repeatedly making mistakes. They don't realize the seriousness and importance of setting up an estate plan that will allow the heirs to receive the assets in the way the family wanted them to be received. One that will minimize the taxes and expenses incurred upon their demise, and prevent the government from taking as much as half of the assets in the form of estate taxes!

It's bad enough that many retirees don't even have a will. And the ones who do have a will, have one that's outdated. It doesn't reflect their current circumstances and wishes, doesn't contain provisions if they became disabled or incapacitated, and needs to be reviewed and incorporated with other documents.

Again, why go through all the trouble of saving and accumulating and managing your estate if, upon your death, the government and attorneys end up walking away with half or more? And, your family has to wait for months or years to receive the assets left after taxes? Or, having assets go to people that you never wanted the assets to go to?

Again, planning is the answer. Planning is the key. We'll talk much more about estate planning in Chapter 11 (How To Protect Your Family And Your Assets When You Pass Away).

Now that we've stated these six dangers and discussed them briefly, we hope we're setting the stage for what's ahead. We hope we're starting to get your mind working on the many things you are doing...or not doing and how your financial health can be in jeopardy.

We hope we are provoking a lot of questions and thoughts in your mind such as, "Am I set up properly? Have we done the right things? Do we know if our wishes will be carried out? Do we have the best chance to beat inflation? Is our portfolio safe and diversified? Are we paying the lowest amount of taxes we legally can? Will our financial plan allow for inflation and help us maintain our life-style without running out of money before we run out of breath!

If you are asking yourself some or all of these questions, that's good. That's what this book is all about.

So, think about it. And again, here are the six ways you can run out of money:

1) **Pay too much in taxes**
2) **Incur catastrophic medical expenses**
3) **Inflation**
4) **Bad investments**
5) **Lawsuits**
6) **Poor estate plan**

Now let's get to the details.

Chapter 4

THE TRUTH ABOUT INFLATION
THE NUMBERS DON'T LIE

ℬ

The subject matter of this particular chapter is not one that needs a great deal of introduction. We're talking about inflation or, another way of saying it is: the things you have to buy go up in price over a period of time.

Now there are all kinds of technical explanations of why inflation occurs. There are many scientific theories and economic models that explain how and why prices go up. We can get this information from textbooks, financial journals, published articles and so on. We're going to skip all that stuff for this book because the reality is that for you and your family...

It doesn't really matter why there is inflation.
All you need to know is that it
is there and understand how to deal with it.

It's like trying to understand why and how the sun works, versus understanding how to live your life while the sun is up, and how to live your life while the sun is down. In other words, how to deal with the fact that there is a sun. That's what we're going to cover in this chapter - how to deal with inflation.

There's a very important aspect of inflation that must be discussed. The issue of the government, and how the government relays information about inflation to members of the general public.

Now, there are all kinds of opinions as to if inflation is created by the government; how the government makes inflation worse than it would be otherwise, and all sorts of related topics.

As we said a minute ago, we're not going to get into that here. But we do think it's important to understand the difference between what the government statistics tell you about inflation versus the impact of inflation on your life.

Over the past 80 years or so, the government has created indices that it reports to us every month. These reports tell us how fast prices are going up. Back in 1913, the government developed a measure of inflation called the Consumer Price Index (CPI). The CPI is a government formula that tells the public how high prices have gone up on average in the United States over a month's period of time. It's then converted to an annual rate of inflation.

For example, the government might say that this month the CPI went up 0.4% (4/10 of 1%), which translates to an annual rate of inflation of approximately 4.8%. They might also tell us that in May, inflation rose 4/10 of 1% for the month, but because of lower figures in previous months, the average annual rate of inflation for this year is actually running at 3.7%, not 4.8% as you would assume.

Now, we are not sure exactly how important or relevant it is for you to understand how the government calculates the Consumer Price Index. In the interest of keeping this book informative and not boring, we won't go into the detailed formulas of how this is done.

We think the simplest explanation, the one that will serve us best in this book, is that the government takes various categories of products and services of a limited nature (in fact, there are a select number of categories they report on) and then takes the average increase in prices on those items, using its formulas. These include housing prices, oil prices, and so forth.

So, what's the problem with the CPI? First of all, since the government uses only a limited number of items in calculating the CPI, the result doesn't necessarily reflect the reality of what you're facing when you buy things on a daily or regular basis.

For example, housing prices may be down on the nationwide average, which would bring the CPI down, but that may be the only sector of our economy that is going down when other areas of our lives may be increasing substantially in cost.

If you're not buying a house, the fact that housing prices went down has no bearing on your life, and what you pay for everything else.

This happens all the time. In fact, I can remember one month when a report said that inflation was running at 0.4% (4/10 of 1%), which would translate to about a 4.8% annual rate of inflation. But, they cautioned, we shouldn't pay too much attention to this, because if you took out the jump in food and energy prices, the index would have only been 0.1% (1/10 of1%)!

This can be somewhat misleading. By telling us to ignore the fact that gas and food prices went sky high it would appear that the increase in the cost of living isn't too bad this month.

However, in order for that number to be meaningful in our lives we need to not have bought food or gasoline that month! To us, this is misleading. The costs of eating and driving cannot be ignored.

Another problem with the CPI is that because it is based on a formula that was developed years ago, it doesn't necessarily mean the formula is correct, nor does it takes into account all the variables that we face today as consumers.

Yet because so many things that we think about in our financial lives revolve around how the government reports inflation to us, this can cause serious problems.

Let's take, for example, the story of Grandma Hannah.

Grandma Hannah was a retiree in 1965. When her husband passed away he left her with a relatively modest pension from the railroad, a Social Security retirement benefit, an almost-paid-for home, and a modest life insurance policy.

In 1965 when she retired, she was receiving a little over $400 a month. She had about $15,000 in the bank, and a mortgage payment of only $97 a month. Her car payment was only $21 a month and her other fixed expenses such as food, utilities, insurance, health costs, etc. only ran about $175-200 a month.

When she retired, Grandma Hannah actually had a small surplus cash flow each month (around an extra $50 a month), money in the bank, and a very secure and peaceful retirement in front of her. Or so she thought!

But then things really changed. Grandma Hannah was in great health, and ten years after her retirement at age 75, she still had basically the same $400 a month coming in, but her expenses had increased to the point where she was running a negative cash flow (spending more than she took in).

Her savings had decreased because she had gone on a few vacations, helped a few of her grandkids with some education costs, paid for part of a wedding, and so on.

But, she was still basically okay. She moved into a retirement home. Her monthly expenses were up to around $700 per month. This negative $300 per month in cash flow didn't seem too bad since she had funds in her bank account to cover the shortfall.

Now we move ahead ten years to 1985. Grandma Hannah is 85, still in really good health, and in financial trouble.

Her bank accounts are at zero. She's living in the retirement home, still in decent health but failing, and having to depend on the grandkids to put in money each month to pay her bills and take care of her.

If she needed anything, the family had to buy it for her. The $400 a month she was getting at age 65, which was OK at the time, was nowhere near enough at age 85!!

Grandma Hannah committed the sin of enjoying good health, and believing that she would be okay in retirement. In fact, inflation had wiped her out.

Now, let's talk a little bit more about how Grandma Hannah's story relates to the government's so-called measure of inflation, and the reality of what Grandma Hannah faced and what we are all facing as well.

According to the U.S. Department Of Labor, Bureau Of Labor Statistics, since 1965, inflation has averaged 4.38% per year.

That's what Uncle Sam says.

Let's take a look at nursing home costs.

If you want to talk about a difference between what Uncle Sam says, and what reality says, let's see how nursing home costs have risen. (We briefly discussed this in the Introduction.)

In 1964, the monthly cost of a top end, high quality nursing home was about $250 a month. (No, that's not a typo. You are reading that correctly.)

$250 a month in 1964. Over, $7,000 a month in 2011 (depending on where you live). In some urban areas, the costs exceed $10,000 a month! Let's use the average cost of $7,000 a month for discussion's sake.

Nursing home costs have risen at an annual rate of 8% per year! This is more than DOUBLE what the government says inflation is running!

Do you ever hear the government talking about these facts:

1. At the same rate of increase, a nursing home stay will cost $155,424 per year (based on the 8% yearly increase in cost) only ten years from now.

2. You will be responsible for those expenses.

As the graying of America continues (That's the Baby Boom generation getting older), the pressure on prices at quality long term care facilities will continue to increase causing the rates to increase at an even higher rate than those we just discussed.

As we said earlier, the cost of long-term medical care is truly the Achilles heal in most of the retirement plans that we see today. We'll talk more about this later. For now, we just want you to be aware of how bad REAL inflation is, and what it might mean to you!

Let's take college education as another example. In 1976, the cost of a four-year, public, state university in most parts of the country was around $2,000, maybe $3,000 in more expensive schools. Today, according to the Princeton Review, a New York-based education services company that regularly analyzes data from approximately 650 colleges and universities estimates the average cost of tuition in 2011 to be $14,333 for in-state, and $25,200 annually for out-of-state. And the average private college is $34,132 annually.

The cost for a 4 year in-state college is up 37% from what it was just 10 years ago. Nothing added or improved, yet the cost continue to skyrocket.

Same college, same dorm, same books (maybe updated versions), but basically nothing better or different. If you look at the Consumer Price Index and multiply 4.38% out over a 30-year period, the price of a college should only be about $8,000.

Let's take another area like your home. In 1968, the median price of a home in the U.S., according to the National Association of Realtors, was $20,100. Today, the median price of a house is $210,000. Using the CPI factor from Uncle Sam, the median price of a house should only be $98,300! But, the real rate of inflation has brought that cost up way more than what the government says. In fact, housing prices have jumped more than 100% higher than the CPI would have you believe!

The same thing is true of gasoline. Remember when gasoline was only 29 cents a gallon? We now pay $3.89 a gallon today to fill up our car.

We could go on making examples all day long, but we think you get the point.

The point is, what the government tells us about inflation and what really is happening are two different things.

In fact, they are so different, that in our viewpoint, the CPI is a meaningless piece of information. We don't pay any attention to it at all.

We can't go into the department store and tell them they have to charge us less for our clothes because, according to the government, the price should only be about half of what they're charging!

The other thing that's very important to understand is that different types of items have different amounts of inflation. Some go up much faster than others.

Medical care and college costs, for example, are significantly more inflated every year than other costs.

Even a general category, like food, may have certain items that explode in price over a period of time because of shortages, increased production costs, etc. (remember when sugar tripled in price literally overnight?)

All this can be summarized by saying there is more inflation than we realize. If we don't plan for it and allow our retirement plan to have a built-in inflation factor; if we don't plan our investments to include a generous amount of inflation to our costs, our retirement plan isn't going to work.

Let's carry some of these figures forward to find out what this really means to you.

For example, as of this writing, we mentioned a few moments ago that gas is $3.89 a gallon. In 1971, if you had told someone that gas would run $3.89 a gallon, they would have thought it would be too expensive to drive a car.

If you had told someone in 1968 that his or her $20,100 house would be selling for $218,900 today, they would have thought you were crazy! (In some places, that $20,100 house has sold for more than $300,000!) Even after the real estate crash of 2008-2011.

When you had a baby 30 years ago and spent about $720 on doctors and hospital fees, you would have thought someone was a lunatic if they told you it would cost $7,000-$8,000 to have the same baby today! And if there are any serious complications, the costs can easily exceed $1 million dollars today.

The national average for medical inflation is over 14% per year.

See, Grandma Hannah didn't realize how bad things were, because she was living her life day-by-day and didn't see the jumps in prices all at once. It just sneaked up on her! Will inflation sneak up on you?

That $3.89 gallon of gas we bought today, based on a realistic inflation figure of at least 3% per year, will cost us $5.38 in ten years, and $7.23 in twenty years.

Imagine it costing over $200 or $300 to fill up your car!

The monthly premium on your health insurance that might cost you $1,000 a month could be $3,700 per month in ten years if it rises with the current rate of medical inflation of 14%.

The car that you bought for $20,000 with a monthly payment of $310 might cost $30,000 with a monthly payment of $450, ten years from now, and more than double that in twenty years. Can you imagine paying $850 per month for a car payment, just to get an average, nothing-fancy type of car?

Well, it's no easier for you to accept paying that high of a monthly car payment than it was for Grandma Hannah to accept that her $97 month rent would turn into a $700 month fee at the retirement center for her to have a place to live.

It's difficult to imagine a basic car costing $40,000, a dinner at McDonalds costing $15 per person, or paying $10 for a box of cereal.

20

But you had better stop thinking those things aren't possible because someday they will become a reality. Slowly and surely your budget will increase. It can be frightening if you dwell upon it. Nevertheless, just because it's scary doesn't mean you can't take action and do something about it.

So, what do we do? How do we deal with inflation?

Now that we understand it's there and we understand how devastating it's going to be, we're going back to our old friend planning as the solution.

So how do we start planning for inflation?

The first thing we have to do is figure out what our monthly budget is in today's dollars, and come up with a realistic number of how much after-tax income we need to live on, right now.

You have to pick one or more inflation rates, and see how much this same monthly budget will cost 5, 10, 15, 20, 25 years from now...to have the same exact lifestyle based on the inflation rates that you pick.

Then, you have to take a look at your investment portfolio plus your current sources of income such as your salary, pension, Social Security, and so on, that you're receiving now. You have to figure out what you're actually getting in interest and the return on your investments. This will tell you what your cash flow is today.

Then, we'll let the computer figure out how much you need to save and/or what you need to earn on average on your investments and/or how much you have to cut your life-style in order to make the whole thing work.

Think about it:

- **Inflation means "things you have to buy go up in price over a period of time."**

- **The Consumer Price Index is an inappropriate government formula for financial planning purposes.**

- **Grandma Hannah committed the sin of enjoying good health and believing she would be okay in retirement, when, in fact, inflation had wiped her out.**

- **At the current rate of inflation, a nursing home stay could cost $19,000 a month in ten years. The government will not pay for this. Nursing home costs are rising at twice the "official" inflation rate.**

- **Inflation can wipe out your purchasing power at any income level. It does not discriminate!**

Chapter 5

WHAT THE IRS DOESN'T WANT YOU TO KNOW!

ℰℴ

The IRS. Three letters that bring concern into the minds of all. The tax collector. A modern day version of the Sheriff of Nottingham Forest.

Paying taxes is an act that people have hated since the beginning of mankind. All through history, you can find story- after-story and tale-after-tale of people fighting the tax collectors.

In fact, there's a country you might be aware of that was founded with the slogan "No more taxation without representation." (Sound familiar?)

Well, these days, most of us do have taxation without representation. There is very little you can say or do, that will affect what tax laws are in place, or how the tax laws are created.

What you CAN do is understand how tax laws work, understand how tax planning works, and be aware of the options that you have and can use to legitimately, legally and safely reduce your taxes.

We mentioned in Chapter 3 that even saving as little as $200 a month over a period of years can be worth tens of thousands of dollars of extra money in your pocket.

We also want to re-emphasize that you have absolutely nothing to fear from the taxman if you follow the laws. Many people tell us they don't want to do any tax planning or take advantage of any tax strategies because they are worried about "getting audited."

Well, you may get audited at some point - who can tell? When you have done nothing illegal, followed the tax laws exactly as written, used the IRS' own tax rules, there isn't too much that can happen besides using up your time with an audit. Remember, they can't do anything when you follow the law.

In a famous court case decades ago, Justice Learned Hand, when issuing his opinion in favor of the taxpayer, said that taxpayers not only have the right, but the duty, to use every legal strategy available to them to reduce their taxes.

Taxpayers are not required to pay any more tax than the lowest amount the law demands. This theory, and way of thinking, must become a way of life.

As you plan for retirement, you must plan out your taxes and reduce them as much as possible. No matter what stage you are in life, no matter what you are doing, we can't imagine why anyone would want to pay more taxes then required by law! Since we see so many people overpaying their taxes, it must come from not understanding the tax laws. Not understanding how tax planning works, or mere procrastination and lethargy. We're going to put an end to that now!

We're going to show you how you can save taxes, give you some concrete ideas on how to reduce the taxes you pay, and be in a position to put more money in your pocket every month instead of Uncle Sam's.

Let's start off with a brief discussion of what tax planning really is.

Tax planning involves three things:

1) **discovering** the different strategies you can use to make wise choices and educated decisions concerning the tax strategies you want to implement;
2) **understanding** them fully; and finally,
3) **integrating** your tax situation with your entire financial plan.

As we've mentioned about financial planning in general, everything you do in one area of your financial life will affect all the others. Nowhere is this truer than in the tax area. There is nothing you can do, financially speaking, that does not have an effect on your taxes.

- If you keep your money in the bank, that affects your taxes.
- If you take your money out of the bank and put it somewhere else, that affects your taxes.
- If you sell stocks, that affects your taxes.
- If you buy a house, that affects your taxes.
- If you sell a house, that affects your taxes.
- If you set up certain trusts and wills for your estate, that affects your taxes.
- If you make gifts, that affects your taxes.
- If you have a part-time or full-time job, that affects your taxes.
- If you own any kind of business, that affects your taxes.

Every activity, financially-speaking, will be somewhere on those tax forms.

Since tax planning and investment planning are so intertwined, they must be done together, in concert, so every decision you make will be integrated and coordinated with the other areas of your financial life.

The first tax strategy we're going to talk about is tax deferral.

1. Tax Deferral

Tax deferral is the concept of having earnings on your investments not be subject to current taxation, but only be taxed when you take money out of the investment at some point in the future.

Let's take a look at an example of how powerful tax deferral can really be.

Ed and Bob both had $250,000 to invest. Ed decided to put his money in a 3% CD at the local bank. Bob decided to put his money in a guaranteed fixed annuity that will also pay 3%. Furthermore, let's assume that both Ed and Bob are in the 25% tax bracket.

Ed made $7,500 (3% of $250,000) each year, but has to pay $1,875 (25% of $7,500) in taxes each year on his earnings. Ed will never see that money again and will never be able to use it for his benefit. Ed's asset is really only growing by 2.25% (3% minus 25% in taxes) each year. If Ed kept his CD, paid tax each year as he has been, Ed would end up with $391,127 at the end of twenty years after paying all taxes. Not a bad sum.

Because Bob invested his assets in a tax deferred annuity, Bob doesn't have to pay any current income taxes on his earnings. Therefore, his assets really do grow by 3% tax deferred. If Bob holds the asset for the same twenty years, his balance will be $451,528. However, Bob never paid any taxes on the growth of $201,528. If he were to cash in the annuity, he would have to pay all of the taxes on the growth. In keeping the comparison fair… let's assume he could cash it all in at a 25% tax bracket, (for example purposes) he would pay a tax of $50,382. This would leave him with $401,045 after-tax (But keep in mind, in the unlikely event Bob did cash out all at once, he would be put into a higher tax bracket).

The bottom line is because Bob controlled his taxes, he was able to make an extra $9,918, after-tax!

By controlling taxes you can make substantially more money. This is the whole reason that IRAs and pension plans are so popular. You don't have to pay any taxes until you withdraw the money, which hopefully will be at a lower tax rate in the future. The larger the growth rate and the larger your tax rate, the more important deferral is.

There are many ways of deferring the tax on your assets. Annuities, life insurance, IRAs, 401(k)s and 403(b)s all provide tax deferral. These are just some of the legal programs that allow the owners not to pay taxes on the earnings until they withdraw them from the plan.

2. Charitable Remainder Trusts (CRT)

How would you like to be able to sell an asset that's gone up in value, pay $0 income tax (capital gains tax) no matter how large the profit, and be able to keep earning income from investment of the proceeds of the sale for the rest of your, and your family's lives?

You can also take charitable deductions and be able to have a big chunk of money go to charities at your death without your family losing any money. Sound interesting? What we've just described is a Charitable Remainder Trust (CRT).

We will tell you a story about Julia and Bill. They were a couple in their early 70's in great health with lots of kids and grandkids. Years ago, they bought some land way out in the country for $10,000 thinking they might build on it some day. The years passed and they never paid much attention to the land and, for various reasons, never did anything with it.

As progress moved outside the main part of town, they soon discovered their little piece of $10,000 land was in the path of development, or a gold mine, you might say. As the development came closer and closer to their land, the price of the land started rising in value. Julia and Bill really didn't want to sell the land because 1) they didn't want to pay the taxes on the profit and 2) they didn't know what they would do with the money anyway. The land just sat there.

When they came in for retirement planning, it was pointed out that this land (which they estimated was now worth about $1 million) wasn't doing them any good. They weren't receiving any income. Their property taxes were going through the roof. They were advised to have liability insurance because of the risk of teenagers partying there. We told them that they should consider selling it.

Bill and Julia protested and said income taxes would kill them. They had talked with their accountant who said the profit would be close to $1 million and they could expect to pay about $150,000 in capital gains taxes from the sale of the land. The money left over would be a nice chunk of cash, but the thought of pouring $150,000 down the drain really bothered them.

We asked them if they had heard of a Charitable Remainder Trust. (CRT) After we explained it to them, they were very excited and set one up. Here's what happened.

Julia and Bill set up a Charitable Remainder Trust naming their church and the church school as beneficiaries. They were named co-trustees of the Trust, and the property was re-titled and donated to the CRT and owned by the CRT.

The act of donating this property irrevocably (meaning it could never be changed) generated a huge charitable deduction. (The complications involved in the calculation will be omitted for purposes of simplicity.)

The donation of $1 million worth of land generated over a $300,000 tax deduction which, spread out over the next few years, could save them as much as $100,000 in income taxes.

That's not the best part. The best part is when the Trust took title to the property, Julia and Bill, as Trustees for the Trust, sold the property to a developer and received $1 million.

The $1 million went into the Trust and was now sitting as a cash investment of the Trust.

**The capital gains tax paid upon the sale
of an asset with a million dollar profit was exactly $0!
Yes, that's right. Zero capital gains tax.**

Since the Trust owned the property, and the Trust was a Charitable Trust, it was a tax-exempt entity, and therefore, any sale of assets inside the Trust was completely free of capital gains tax.

Now, instead of having $850,000 left out of $1million, they have $1 million left out of $1 million because they paid $0 capital gains tax. (They did not lose the $150,000 they would have lost had they sold it the usual way most people would have sold it.)

It's still not over. They also saved $100,000 in income taxes over the next several years with charitable deductions, and they saved the original $150,000 in capital gain taxes for a total of $250,000 in saved taxes.

And, they still have $1 million sitting in the bank that they control. Now, they can never get the principal out of this Trust, but they do get the income that the Trust generates for the remainder of their lives.

They invested the $1 million with a careful investment plan and were able to average 7% on the money with basically little risk. They are earning $70,000 income a year off the $1 million in the Trust.

Keep in mind, had they sold the land outright they would have $850,000 left after paying taxes. If they earned 7% on that $850,000, they would only be receiving $59,500 in income, or $20,000 less per year. This is because they would have lost the ability to earn interest on the $200,000 that would have been paid in taxes.

The last thing Julia and Bill did was set up a Wealth Replacement Trust funded with a second–to–die life insurance policy for $1 million. So, when they pass away, their family will still get the $1 million they would have had if they still owned the land. But instead of the land providing the money, the life insurance will provide the money. They were able to buy the life insurance policy using a very small portion of the tax savings they realized from selling the land asset through the Trust.

And, on top of all that, the $1million dollars will be free from both income and estate taxes!

Is this amazing or what?

Charitable Remainder Trusts are one of the best tax planning techniques ever to come out of Congress and have been around for decades. They are perfectly legal. Yet hardly anyone understands or uses them. They are a great example of a sound tax strategy that can save you money even if the assets you want to sell are only worth $100,000 instead of $1 million. Just reduce Julia and Bill's numbers by ten.

Do you think the IRS will tell you about Charitable Remainder Trusts? Has your accountant or attorney told you about Charitable Remainder Trusts? Most likely, no. It is a little known technique that many advisors are not that familiar with.

We think it's about time for every American and every retiree to have the opportunity to understand and use this idea if it fits their situation.

If so, don't forget that you MUST set up a CRT ONLY with the advice and counsel of your tax and legal advisors! Anything related to income tax and charitable donations must be done exactly right, and the rules change frequently! This is not a do-it–yourself project.

3. Change Your Assets To Earn Tax-Free Income

There are many areas of the economy where Congress has decided to give tax breaks. Certain programs, if you invest in them, will give you tax-free income.

For example, did you know that the cash value of many life insurance policies can be taken out tax-free? Yes, it's true. The money grows tax-free and the gain can be taken out tax-free through borrowing. Many people are unaware of that.

Many real estate investments can provide you tax-advantaged income. Depreciation and other expenses can offset the money you receive as rent, so the earnings you receive monthly or quarterly may be partially or even completely offset so the cash flow could end up not being taxed!

Municipal bonds, of course, provide tax-free income and may fit into your portfolio. However, too much tax-free income may cause your Social Security to be taxed. Remember we said that one action might trigger another adverse reaction. Planning can avoid these surprises.

There are numerous ways you can receive tax-free income instead of purely taxable income.

Are you starting to see why keeping your money in the bank or mutual funds that pay taxable dividends may not be in your best interest?

Have you ever thought about saving money in equity indexed annuities where all the earnings are deferred inside the annuity? You pay no tax on the dividends or gains until you actually take out the money. The proceeds are passed to your heirs free from probate. And, your heirs can be guaranteed to receive the highest value your account reached on the policy anniversary during your lifetime regardless of where the market is on the day you die!

We could write volumes on tax savings strategies, but we won't go into the technical details and bore you or confuse the issues. We hope you can see that there are many ways to save money in income taxes that you could be taking advantage of. If you are like most of the clients we see, you aren't taking advantage of any of these perfectly legal strategies to keep your hard-earned money.

One final story to share with you as we close on this chapter.

Vince and Betty, a couple in their late 70's, were referred to us for financial planning by their cousins. When we reviewed their financial situation, we saw their total investment portfolio consisted of $300,000 in CDs. The earnings on the CDs at that time were approximately 6%, or $18,000 per year. Based on their tax bracket, this $18,000 of taxable earnings was costing them approximately $5,400 per year in federal taxes.

The sad thing was, this $5,400 was paid needlessly because Vince and Betty did not use that money to live on. Betty had a trust fund she inherited from her parents and Vince had a big pension and Social Security income. Their house was paid for, their cars were paid for. Their kids were grown and on their own.

Basically, they were in great financial shape except they were paying $5,400 in taxes they didn't have to pay. We showed them some different options for their planning including fixed rate and equity indexed annuities.

After seeing the difference these savings vehicles made in their plan, they decided to go ahead and reinvest their CD money into these other options.

When we saw them again a few years later to review their financial plan, Vince and Betty were still in good health and enjoying their retirement years. They told us, "We just wanted to thank you so much for pointing out other options to us and how to save $5,400 a year in taxes. We've been using that money we're not paying in taxes to set up a scholarship fund at Vince's Alma Mater for underprivileged kids so they can afford to go to school. We never would have been able to do that without your help."

See, that's the beauty about saving tax money. The money can go anywhere. It can be used for charitable purposes, your family, vacations, a house addition, to pay bills, whatever. Anything is better than paying needless taxes!

Bear in mind that tax planning is not just for the rich, it's for everybody, and you must - we repeat, MUST - discover your options and use your options to save that tax money and put it to better use.

We can't get rid of your taxes altogether, but we can help you get rid of some taxes. This is a key point we hope you spend a lot of time thinking about.

Think about it.

Tax planning involves:

1) **discovering** the different strategies you can use to make wise choices and educated decisions concerning the tax strategies you want to implement;

2) **understanding** them fully; and finally,

3) **integrating** your taxes with your entire financial plan.

Tax strategies include:

- **Tax Deferral**
- **Charitable Remainder Trusts (CRTs)**
- **Repositioning Your Assets For Tax-Free or Tax Deferred Income**

Chapter 6

FIRST THINGS FIRST –
HOW TO KNOW WHERE YOU ARE TODAY

ℰↄ

The first step you have to take in retirement planning is to figure where you are today. In any journey, you'll never get to where you want to go without knowing where you're starting from...and where you want to go! (We'll talk about where you want to go in the next chapter.)

As we've already discussed, the journey of planning has to begin somewhere. And that somewhere is an understanding of everything you have going on right now.

An "inventory" and "diagnosis" of your current situation, you might say.

For example, if you want to increase your return on invested dollars, you first have to know how much money you have, and what your after-tax rate of return is on that money.

If you just started changing things without knowing what returns you're getting now, how could you make an educated decision about what to change, what to change it to, and how much to change? The answer is that you couldn't.

We know it sounds silly to say that you must know these things first before making decisions. It might sound silly, but we cannot tell you how many people we see who have made all kinds of decisions without knowing what they were doing before they made the changes.

They had no specific idea what their current situation was, yet made changes anyway. Sometimes they got lucky and improved their situation making changes blindly. More often than not, they ended up in worse shape.

And, many times...there's no way to tell! How can you tell if you are better or worse if you have no idea what you're comparing your new results to?

It all comes down to this:

The First Step In Retirement Planning
Is To Know Where You Are Today!

You need to know things like:

1. Your current cash flow.
2. Your expenses.
3. Your investment amounts and rates of return.
4. Your liabilities. (How much you owe.)
5. Maturity dates of CDs, annuities, etc.
6. Who owns what.
7. What you paid for things like stocks, bonds, etc.
8. Your current tax situation. (How much you have taken out for taxes, or how much you pay in estimated payments, what your deductible expenses are.)
9. Your current insurance coverage.
10. Any employer provided benefits like insurance, pensions,401(k)s, etc.
11. How much your personal assets are worth. (Your home(s), car(s), jewelry, etc.)
12. Any government benefits received. (Social Security, pensions, etc.)
13. Your current estate planning arrangements. (Wills, Trusts, etc.)
    And so on.

As you can see, you need to gather together a complete list of everything you have going on. You can't get a handle on what to do until you know what you have. You may have to dig through some old shoeboxes, safety deposit boxes, files, drawers, and so on to find everything.

You may have to make some calls to get updated information on some things. You may have to call your broker to find out what you paid for a stock. You may have to call your accountant to get a copy of your last year's tax return. Or whatever.

You may have to guess on some items, because you cannot find the answers anywhere or from anyone. While you may not get 100% of all this stuff together, getting as much as possible is better than doing nothing! To help you with this, we've included two useful items on the following pages.

We've given you a simple cash flow worksheet to fill out so you can see what you're really spending. While not all of you will want to do this, we think it's critical to know what you're spending.

The second item is a checklist of things you may need to collect to get a handle on what you have currently.

While these forms are intended to be pretty comprehensive, if you have things not included in them, you of course, can add them in the places marked "Other."

If you never do any retirement planning, if you never take any actions to change what you're doing, if you never find out what other options you have available to you, you should at least get a handle on where you are today!

Just going through the exercise of getting your information together, seeing what you have and don't, and knowing where everything is, is worth it in-and-of itself.

Having a grasp on what you've accumulated throughout the years is great to know.

You'll feel more organized, be more objective, and be in more control.

Remember that this isn't an exercise to criticize yourself, or to bring up things you maybe would rather forget. It's simply the time to "take stock," to get an inventory, to see where you are today!

We promise you'll be glad you took the time to do this, no matter what you decide to do about the information you gather!

So go out to the garage and start opening up those folders. Take a trip to the bank, and get going!

We have included several forms at the end of this chapter to help you get organized. These forms ask for most of the data you will need in order to begin the planning process. Your financial professional can help you complete these forms, if necessary.

DATA & DOCUMENT CHECKLIST

Note: Check the items applicable to your situation and complete all pertinent information for all family members.   If you're not sure what to complete, just complete everything!

APPLICABLE	OBTAINED	**PERSONAL INFORMATION**
_____	_____	Family names, birthdays, year(s) in school
_____	_____	Social Security numbers
_____	_____	Attorney's name, address, phone
_____	_____	Tax Preparer's name, address, phone
_____	_____	Premarital agreements, separation agreements, divorce decrees, wills/codicils trust agreements

EMPLOYMENT INFORMATION

_____	_____	Last 2 detailed paycheck or pension \stubs
_____	_____	Summary plan descriptions for:
_____	_____	Group life insurance
_____	_____	Group medical/dental insurance
_____	_____	Group disability
_____	_____	Pension/profit sharing plan(s)
_____	_____	ESOP/stock option plan(s)
_____	_____	Thrift/401k plan(s)
_____	_____	Deferred compensation plan(s)
_____	_____	Tax sheltered annuities/TSA's
_____	_____	Account statements (for above plans)
_____	_____	Beneficiary designations (for above plans)
_____	_____	Annual benefits summary statements

INDIVIDUAL INSURANCE POLICIES
(including recent premium, loan and dividend statements)

_____	_____	Life
_____	_____	Annuities
_____	_____	Disability
_____	_____	Long-term Care Insurance
_____	_____	Hospitalization/major medical
_____	_____	Automobile
_____	_____	Other property
_____	_____	Liability Umbrella

INVESTMENT RECORDS

Personal financial statement
Account statements for:
Banks, CDs, (yield & maturity date)
Brokerage accounts; purchase price
Mutual fund/dividend reinvest accounts
IRA/Keogh/Pension accounts
Partnership Agreements
Loan & mortgage agreements
balances, original amounts, interest rate
Savings Bonds
Prospectus/offering memoranda
Transaction confirmations, K-1's
Personal property values (furniture, autos, misc.)
IRA/Keogh plan description (5500's)
Real estate; original cost, market value, Date acquired, original mortgage
Real estate rental properties (same as above plus rents, expenses & insurance)

TAX RETURNS

Federal & state income tax for last 3 years
Federal gift tax returns
Details on quarterly tax estimates
Income & deduction estimated for
Current year tax

MISCELLANEOUS

Info. on inheritances or anticipated
Completed budget worksheet
Checkbooks & check registers

BUSINESS OWNERS

Copies of corporate returns, federal & state
Copies of partnership agreements or
Articles of Incorporation
Copies of latest business financial stmts
Copies of buy and sell, stock redemption, split dollar and other agreements
Value of business and stock or
Ownership percentage
Qualified, retirement deferred
Compensation plan(s), docs. & stmts.
Business insurance coverages

34

CASH FLOW WORKSHEET

For: _____ Date: _____

INCOME	MONTHLY	ANNUAL
SALARY (H)	_____	_____
SALARY (W)	_____	_____
PENSION (H)	_____	_____
PENSION (W)	_____	_____
SOCIAL SECURITY (H)	_____	_____
SOCIAL SECURITY (W)	_____	_____
OTHER	_____	_____

GROSS INCOME	_____	_____

DEDUCTIONS FOR:		
FEDERAL TAXES	_____	_____
STATE TAXES	_____	_____
SOCIAL SECURITY TAXES	_____	_____
GROUP BENEFITS	_____	_____
OTHER	_____	_____

TOTAL DEDUCTIONS	_____	_____

FIXED EXPENDITURES:

	MONTHLY	ANNUAL
MORTGAGE OR RENT	_____	_____
REAL ESTATE TAXES	_____	_____
LIFE INSURANCE	_____	_____
HEALTH INSURANCE	_____	_____
DISABILITY INS.	_____	_____
AUTOMOBILE INS.	_____	_____
HOMEOWNER'S INS.	_____	_____
LIABILITY INSURANCE	_____	_____
LONG-TERM CARE INS.	_____	_____
ALIMONY/CHILD SUPPORT	_____	_____
TUITION/EDUCATION	_____	_____
GROCERIES	_____	_____
GAS/ELECTRIC/WATER/ETC.	_____	_____
TELEPHONE	_____	_____
CAR PAYMENTS	_____	_____
OTHER	_____	_____

TOTAL FIXED EXPENSES _____ _____

DISCRETIONARY EXPENDITURES:

CLOTHING/CLEANING _____ _____
MEDICAL/DRUGSTORE/
  DENTAL _____ _____
AUTO REPAIR/
  MAINTENANCE _____ _____
HOME REPAIR/
  MAINTENANCE _____ _____
MEALS OUT/
  ENTERTAINMENT _____ _____
GAS/PUBLIC
  TRANSPORTATION _____ _____
GIFTS FOR RELATIVES _____ _____
VACATIONS/TRAVEL _____ _____
DONATIONS _____ _____
OTHER _____ _____

TOTAL DISC. EXP. _____ _____

TOTAL EXPENDITURES _____ _____

NET SAVING
 (BORROWING)* _____ _____

_____ _____

*(Gross Income + Deductions) – (Total Expenditures) = Net Savings

PERSONAL EXPENSE SUMMARY

NAME:		DATE:

	Monthly	OR	Annually		Monthly	OR	Annually
EDUCATION EXPENSES				**HOUSEHOLD CON'T.**			
Tuition, Books				2nd Mortgage (Prin/Interest Only)			
Room & Board				Rent			
Travel				Association/Condo Fees			
				Gas/Electric/Oil			
ESTIMATED TAXES				Cable TV			
(Do not include Federal Tax)				Groceries			
Intangible Tax				Child Care			
Property Tax				Clothing			
				Telephone-LD, Local, Cell, Pager			
INSURANCE				Household Maintenance			
Homeowners				Water, Sewer, Garbage			
Automobile				Home Furnishings			
Umbrella				Pest Control			
Medical/Hospital				Lawn Care/Maintenance			
Life				Domestic Help			
Dental/Vision				Security System			
Long Term Care				Pool			
Disability							
Termite Bond				**GIFTS**			
				Charity/Offerings			
RECREATION				Birthdays			
Dining Out				Holidays (C'mas, Han., Val., Mom)			
Movies, Entertainment				Anniversaries			
Vacations/Retreats				Church/Synagogue			
Sporting Events							
Hobbies (Golf, Tools, etc.)				**MISCELLANEOUS**			
Home Entertaining				Medical			
Health/Sports Club Dues				Dental/Vision			
Baby Sitting				Personal Care, Hair, etc.			
				Professional Dues			
TRANSPORTATION				Subscriptions, Mags, News			
Auto Loan/Lease				Pet Care			
Gasoline				Allowances			
Maintenance, Repairs				Adult Support			
Auto Tag, Fees				Dry Cleaners			
Public Trans, Parking, Tolls				Internet Access			
				Music Lessons			
HOUSEHOLD				Children's Activities (Camps, etc.)			
1st Mortgage (Prin/Interest Only)							

Grand Total		

CURRENT ANNUAL INCOME

	CLIENT A	CLIENT B	JOINT
SALARY (GROSS)			
ANNUAL SALARY INCREASE %			
BONUS			
DIVIDENDS			
INTEREST			
SOCIAL SECURITY			
NET RENTAL PROPERTY INCOME (LOSS)			
INVESTMENT INCOME			
PENSION			
OTHER			
TOTAL GROSS INCOME(S)			
MARGINAL TAX RATE			
TOTAL NET ANNUAL TAKE HOME INCOME(S)			

EDUCATIONAL GOALS

NAME OF CHILD	PRIVATE Y/N	YEARS BEFORE COLLEGE	CLIENT'S SUPPORT %

DO YOU EXPECT ANY SIGNIFICANT INCREASE IN EITHER YOUR CASH RECEIPTS OR EXPENSES THIS YEAR?   YES___ NO___

DO YOU EXPECT ANY MAJOR INHERITANCE OR LEGAL SETTLEMENTS IN THE NEAR FUTURE?   YES___ NO___

DO YOU ANTICIPATE ANY FINANCIAL DEPENDENCY BY RELATIVES?   YES___ NO___

LIST ANY ASSETS TRANSACTIONS THAT HAVE OCCURRED THIS PAST YEAR THAT WILL AFFECT YOUR TAX LIABILITY THIS YEAR (STOCK, REAL ESTATE SALE, ETC.).

LIFE INSURANCE

COMPANY	TYPE	INSURED	OWNER	BENEFICIARY	FACE AMOUNT	PREMIUM & FREQUENCY	NET CASH VALUE	SMOKER?

DISABILITY/LONG TERM CARE INSURANCE

COMPANY	MONTHLY BENEFITS	HOW LONG UNTIL BENEFITS BEGIN?	LENGTH	COST	PAYER

HEALTH INSURANCE

COMPANY	DEDUCTIBLE	COST	PAYER

SURVIVOR CONSIDERATIONS
AFTER TAX MONTHLY INCOME?
SURVIVOR OBTAIN EMPLOYMENT?   INCOME?
CLIENT A WILL?   STATE?   YEAR?
CLIENT B WILL?   STATE?   YEAR?

DISABILITY CONSIDERATIONS
AFTER-TAX MONTHLY INCOME REQUIREMENTS?
CLIENT A EMPLOYMENT?   EXPECTED INCOME?
CLIENT B EMPLOYMENT?   EXPECTED INCOME?

ASSETS	
CHECKING	
(1) SAVINGS/MONEY MARKET	
(2) SAVINGS/MONEY MARKET	
CD'S: (1) MAT DATE	
(2) MAT DATE	
MUTUAL FUNDS	
BONDS	
STOCKS	
IRA – CLIENT A	
IRA – CLIENT B	
ROTH – CLIENT A	
ROTH – CLIENT B	
RETIREMENT PLAN CLIENT A VESTED AMOUNT	
RETIREMENT PLAN CLIENT B VESTED AMOUNT	
HOME(S) – COST/FMV	
INVESTMENT / REAL ESTATE – COST/FMV	

REITS	
MORTGAGES/NOTES RECEIVABLE	
ANNUITIES	
LTD PARTNERSHIPS	
PERSONAL PROPERTY (JEWELRY, ART, ETC.)	
VALUE OF BUSINESS	
CAR 1	
CAR 2	
OTHER	
TOTAL ASSETS	

LIABILITIES	
HOME 1ST MORTGAGE (RATE____)	
DATE OF ORIGIN (TERM____)	
HOME 2ND MORTGAGE (RATE____)	
DATE OF ORIGIN_____(TERM____)	
2nd HOME 1ST MORTGAGE (RATE____)	
DATE OF ORIGIN_____(TERM____)	
2nd HOME 2ND MORTGAGE (RATE____)	
DATE OF ORIGIN_____(TERM____)	
INVESTMENT PROPERTY (RATE____)	
DATE OF ORIGIN_____(TERM____)	
INVESTMENT PROPERTY (RATE____)	
DATE OF ORIGIN_____(TERM____)	
INVESTMENT PROPERTY (RATE____)	
DATE OF ORIGIN (TERM____)	
REVOLVING CHARGE ACCTS. (RATE____)	
NOTES PAYABLE (RATE____)	
CAR LOAN(S) (RATE____)	
STUDENT LOAN(S) (RATE____)	
FUTURE OBLIGATIONS	
OTHER	
TOTAL LIABILITIES	

NET WORTH	
TOTAL ASSETS	
TOTAL LIABILITIES	
NET WORTH	

Chapter 7

GOAL SETTING MADE EASY:
HOW TO SET GOALS THAT CAN BE REACHED!

ଅଂ

We just finished talking about the first step to proper planning, finding out where you are today. Now we're going to chat about the next part of the equation, setting goals. As we've said, you can't know where you're going if you don't know where you're headed! You can't get to your destination, if you don't know what it is!

We know that sounds like kindergarten-type instructions, but it's a big problem for most people, regardless of their station in life!

Just like taking a trip, you have to know what your destination is, or you won't be too likely to get there.

Most people, retired or not, answer the following question somewhat the same:

What Are Your Financial Goals?

The answers are usually something like:
1. I want to be rich.
2. I want to be secure.
3. I want to be able to sleep at night.
4. I just want enough money to be able to do what I want to without worrying.
5. I want to live in a beautiful house in a nice neighborhood.
6. I want to send my grandchildren to whatever college they want to go to.
7. I want to be able to travel all over the world.
8. I just want to be self sufficient, and not be a burden to my children.
9. I want a million dollars in the bank.

Or whatever. Any of them sound familiar? See, these "goals" are really not financial goals at all. Here's why:

A financial goal isn't a goal unless it includes specific, measurable, quantifiable amounts of money, and it contains a rational reason for that amount of money!

For example, if you say you want to be "rich," that means nothing in reality. What does "rich" mean anyway?

To some readers, "rich" means having an income of $100,000 a month. To others, having an income of $4,000 a month would be "rich." It's all relative.

Some people say they want a "million dollars" in the bank, when they have no idea if that amount is enough for them to feel "rich." If someone wants to live on $10,000 a month, and has a million dollars in the bank earning 3% interest, he or she will be out of money in about 10 years. Is that rich?

What if you are 65 years old, are used to living on $10,000 a month, and all you have is $1 million in the bank, and you are in great health? Are you "rich?"

Some would say you are. You may think you're "poor" because you only have enough money to last until you're 75 based on the life-style you've gotten used to!

What if you have the same $1 million and you only need $2,000 a month to live? Are you "rich" yet? See how variable and subjective these types of "goals" are?

Do you see that what may seem like a fortune to one person, may seem like a pauper's sum to another? And, is anyone wrong for thinking one way or the other?

If you are used to living on $2,000 a month, and are very comfortable, and a family member lives on $8,000 a month, and thinks living on $2,000 a month is awful...are either of you right or wrong? Of course not. Everyone's entitled to his or her opinions and feelings.

Some people may think living in a one-bedroom condo is a "nice house, while others may think a 3-story mansion is a "nice" house.

The important fact is that calling things a name, putting a label on a life-style is meaningless. To have meaningful goals that can be used as objectives you try to reach, your goals must be calculated on a logical, rational, numbers crunching basis!

For example, if you are just about to retire, and you are used to living on $4,000 a month, you cannot tell yourself or your advisors that you want to remain "comfortable" during retirement.

That term "comfortable" doesn't mean much. You need to decide how much money you need to live on to feel "comfortable," then use the dollar amount, adjusted for inflation, as your goal! If you feel you can live on $3,500 a month "comfortably," that goal, adjusted for the increase in the cost of living each year, is your goal!

If you think inflation should be roughly 4% per year, then all you have to do is use a financial calculator or have a professional advisor show you how much you have to earn on your investment capital, allowing for your pension and Social Security, to have the inflated equivalent of $3,500 a month over your expected life span.

Now we've converted a nebulous term like "comfortable," into a meaningful, specific, measurable goal to shoot for!

Then, as time goes by, you can monitor your plan, see if your goal is achievable, and make changes to your plan as necessary.

Do you see how critical it is to get away from naming your goals, and to instead put hard numbers to those goals?

If you want to live in a beautiful house in a nice neighborhood, how much does the house cost? How much are the taxes and maintenance? And so on.

You have to attach numbers to the goals to make them true goals you can shoot for, and measure your progress. So saying you want a "million dollars" now needs to be translated into a real goal.

The real goal would be, "I want enough money in the bank to live on $10,000 a month for 25 years, assuming a 4% inflation rate!"

Now that's a goal. (And the answer will be a lot more than a million dollars. If you earned 4% on your money, you'd need $3,064,610 in the bank to do this!)

So, when you sit down to work on the second part of planning, setting goals, make sure you think of everything in terms of how much does it cost, instead of describing the "goal" with words. Then you'll be on the right track!

If you don't know exactly what you want, that's fine. Try to get a rough idea of what you want and then start with that goal now. If your vision of what you see for yourself gets clearer, then change the goal later on.

It's better to have some goals you're working towards, then no goals at all!

Finally, we know that setting goals may be hard, because the future can be uncertain. But, uncertainty will be with you, whether you set goals or not. So, if you have plans with specific goals, and your plans or goals change, or if the economy or your life change, you will have to adjust your actions accordingly.

Setting goals doesn't guarantee you'll reach them or keep them once you get them.

Having no specific goals assures you'll have a difficult time reaching them, since you don't have any! So, setting goals is a crucial ingredient to financial success!

THINK ABOUT IT... **A financial goal isn't a goal unless it includes specific, measurable, quantifiable amounts of money, and it contains a rational reason for that amount of money.**

Chapter 8

HOW MUCH MONEY DO YOU NEED TO RETIRE SO YOU NEVER OUTLIVE YOUR MONEY?

ജ

This is a scary question. How much money do you really need to retire? How much money do you really need...so you won't outlive your money?

In the old days this question wasn't so difficult. Remember the times when something cost $1 new, and many years later might only cost $1.05? Remember when a buck was a buck? Over the last couple of decades, when rampant inflation has become part of our lives, when a buck isn't even close to a buck...it's a much more difficult question to answer.

If you remember, a few chapters ago we talked about Grandma Hannah and how she ran out of money. How the family had to take care of her in her later years?

We talked about Grandma Hannah and what she didn't know about inflation. We talked about how the government's inept management has caused inflation. That its deficit spending will continue to cause a built-in inflation that is never going away causing many retirees to literally outlive their money.

The increases in lifespan due to dramatic improvements in the health-care system are wonderful. It's great to see people living in their 70s, 80s, 90s, even 100 enjoying excellent health. That's the good news.

The bad news is that it takes lots of money to live.

Sure, money can't solve all your problems, but no one will disagree with the fact that you need to have some to live on. You need money to pay bills, buy groceries, medicine, take care of yourself and yes, even enough money to have cable TV.

Now we've talked about this inflation problem and uncovered the truth about how it affects people. Now we've come to the point where we need to discuss how you plan your finances so that your money won't run out.

For a lot of people this is a very difficult and complicated question. It becomes complex for people because they don't have any idea what their current expenses are, let alone what their expenses will be in the future with inflation taken into account.

Listen to the story of Clara and Bryan.

Clara had been a head nurse at a hospital and was about to retire at age 64. Bryan, age 65, had been, a foreman his whole life and belonged to a union since he was a young man. He had some money put away for retirement in the union pension plan, but between the two of them, they really hadn't saved a ton of money.

They were quite concerned about their situation because Clara had an older Aunt Joan who was in her upper 80s and was living solely on Social Security and food stamps. Joan wasn't sick and didn't require a nursing home but had nowhere near enough money to take care of her needs. Clara and Bryan were very concerned that this would happen to them.

What we told Clara and Bryan and what we're telling you is -

There are no guarantees. There are no perfect answers.

Obviously, no one can really project with 100% accuracy what will happen in the future. But, by the same token, it doesn't mean we can't make a serious attempt to use careful planning and the power of computers to project the future given certain assumptions. We can use sound retirement planning techniques to get a handle on Clara and Bryan's situation today and help them see where they will be in the future...and what to do about it.

The real answer is that YOU have to run the numbers. It's basically a question of mathematics.

Clara and Bryan had a certain amount of money in the bank, a house, a mortgage, a pension, investment income, and Social Security income, etc.

The real job here is to take that information, put it into a computer program, project the rate of inflation, figure out what they will need to live on each month in today's dollars and future dollars, and let the computer tell us what rate of return they need to earn on their money and how long the money will last under different assumptions.

We don't know any other way to do this. You can't do this with a hand-held calculator. You can't just guess with a pencil and a yellow legal pad. You really need to crunch the numbers and see what the projections tell you.

Let's use Clara and Bryan's actual numbers as a case study here to see how their situation looked when they came in, what their initial numbers showed based on what they said they were trying to do. And then we'll look at what we finally recommended they do with the revised plan of action.

44

To start with, their home was worth $255,000 based on comparisons with other home selling prices in the neighborhood. We agreed with them that it was a realistic figure, plus or minus. In reality it doesn't make any difference. Why? Because for a retired couple or an individual who isn't going to sell their home, the actual market value really doesn't make a heck of a lot of difference.

If you're not going to sell the home and reposition the money elsewhere to provide income, we don't count it in our calculations. It's nothing more than an asset you own that may go up in value but is really worthless to you from the standpoint of retirement income.

It's not unusual for us to have to recommend to retirees that they consider purchasing a smaller house or even renting and then repositioning the equity tied up in their house. And sometimes we look at a reverse mortgage to generate extra income.

As you will see in a few minutes, in Clara and Bryan's situation, it was recommended they consider moving to a smaller place because so much of their net worth was tied up in the home. After paying on the mortgage for 25 years, they only had a balance left of $14,500. So they had a lot of money tied up in an asset that really didn't help to produce income.

Now, when we talked to them initially, they were asked if they were to find that they needed some of the equity in their home to produce income, would they consider moving to a smaller place or to a different area?

Sometimes when we ask this question, people tell us they have no intention of ever moving. It's just not going to happen. Which is fine. That's why we do such extensive and detailed interviews. We need clients to tell us what they are willing to consider, and what they're NOT willing to consider.

If we don't know what you really want, what you are willing to change, and what you don't want to change, we can't do a good job helping you.

So, when we asked Clara and Bryan how they felt about this, they responded that they had talked about maybe getting a condo or townhouse since they didn't need a big house any more. And, they added that if the plan showed them that moving to a smaller place would make a difference in their finances, they would seriously consider it.

Here's a summary of what their situation was when they came in to see us:

- $255,000 house with a $14,500 mortgage left. Equity of $240,500, with a profit of $190,000 over what they paid for the house years ago.
- $246,788 in CDs, IRA's, savings bonds, savings accounts, etc.
- A monthly pension of $740 for Bryan and $121 for Clara.

- A monthly Social Security of $788 for Bryan, and $380 for Clara.
- A desire to live on the inflated equivalent of $3,000 per month. (Which was about $1,000 a month less than they lived on when they were working.)
- They were earning a 3% after-tax rate of return on the assets they had invested. (Most of the money was in the bank and in savings bonds and low yielding investments.)

OK. The table and graph on the following pages show that if they just continued to do what they were doing, they would have run out of money at age 78! (See Projection 1)

The only way their money would be able to last longer would be to earn a higher rate of return, or to cut back on their life-style and need for income.

As you can see from the following table, if they were able to earn 12% on their assets, the money would last well into their nineties - a big difference. But trying to earn 12% would cause them to take risks they weren't ready to take. (Projection 2)

(That's a pretty healthy rate of return to shoot for and isn't realistic since they said they didn't want to take the risk of losing their principal.)

Ages		Annual Expenses incl. tax	Less					Annual surplus	Begin. year Account totals
			Earned income	Retirement acc't distr *	Investment acc't distr *	Pensions/ Soc Sec	Other Inc & St Opt		
		1	2	3	4	5	6	7	8
65	64	$36,000			$26,544	$9,456			$246,788
66	65	37,440			12,833	24,607			226,851
67	66	40,419			15,548	24,871			220,437
68	67	42,514			17,374	25,140			211,035
69	68	44,751			19,337	25,414			199,469
70	69	46,660		1,979	18,988	25,693			185,534
71	70	48,607		2,031	20,599	25,978			169,503
72	71	50,623		7,083	22,273	26,267			151,277
73	72	52,722		2,137	24,023	26,562			130,727
74	73	54,910		2,192	25,856	26,862			107,703
75	74	57,189		7,248	27,773	27,168			82,043
76	75	59,564		29,223	2,861	27,479			53,580
77	76	62,631		22,139		27,797		(2,695)	22,139
78	77	62,492				28,120		(34,372)	

Note - CT = client life expectancy age   Sp = spouse life expectancy age

*Investment and Retirement distributions include withdrawals from account trusts to satisfy "Income needed" shortages from Cash Flow report

47

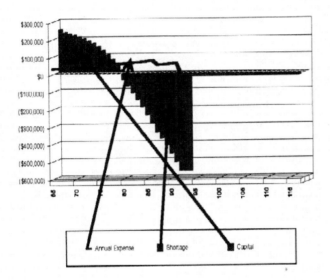

As inflation increases the amount of income needed for your standard of living, there is the potential need to draw increasing amounts out of savings, investments and retirement accounts.

The graph shows how long your capital will last. The objective is to assure that your capital is properly managed so that it will last at least until your life expectancy.

If the capital is depleted before your need for income has ceased, then you will become dependent on your pensions, social security, relatives or public sources. If there is capital remaining when your need for income stops then the remaining capital is available for your heirs.

The line allows you to visualize the annual expenses as compared to your capital accounts.

If the bars dip below the "0" level on the graph, it indicates that you have consumed all your savings, investment and retirement accounts, and your spending requirements have caused a "deficit" spending situation - a need for funds where none exists.

48

Retirement Capital Projection: CLARA AND BRYAN **PROJECTION 2**

Ages		Annual Expenses incl. tax	Less					Annual surplus	Begin year Account totals
			Earned income	Retirement acct distr *	Investment acct distr *	Pensions/ Soc Sec	Other income		
		1	2	3	4	5	6	7	0
65	64	$36,000			$26,544	$9,456			$246,788
66	65	39,798			15,191	24,607			246,673
67	66	40,570			15,699	24,871			259,258
68	67	42,247			17,107	25,140			272,784
69	68	44,095			18,681	25,414			286,355
70	69	45,938		3,009	17,236	25,693			299,795
71	70	47,738		3,357	18,403	25,978			313,093
72	71	49,675		3,745	19,663	26,267			326,291
73	72	51,701		4,178	20,961	26,562			339,228
74	73	53,830		4,660	22,308	26,862			351,774
75	74	56,304		5,196	23,940	27,168			363,781
76	75	58,958		5,793	25,686	27,479			374,803
77	76	61,732		6,427	27,509	27,797			384,538
78	77	64,614		7,163	29,332	28,120			392,649
79	78	67,481		7,940	31,092	28,449			398,890
80	79	70,255		8,798	32,673	28,784			403,039
81	80	73,113		9,743	34,244	29,125			404,952
82	81	76,075		10,785	35,817	29,473			404,277
83	82	79,336		11,931	37,578	29,827			400,593
84	83	84,114		13,190	40,736	30,188			393,212
85	84	89,024		14,474	43,995	30,555			379,999
86	85	93,392		15,866	46,597	30,929			360,113
87	86	69,312		17,372	25,511	22,430			333,367
88	87	66,068		18,997	31,204	15,867			320,861
89	88	72,337		20,745	35,259	16,134			303,137
90	89	75,158		37,541	21,209	16,405			276,788
91	90	74,107		58,878		15,230			244,199
									207,559
111	110								
112	111								
113	112								
114	113								
115	114								
116	115								
117	116								

Note - Cl* = client life expectancy age. Sp* = spouse life expectancy age.

*Investment and Retirement distributions include withdrawals from account totals to satisfy "Income needed" shortages from Cash Flow report.

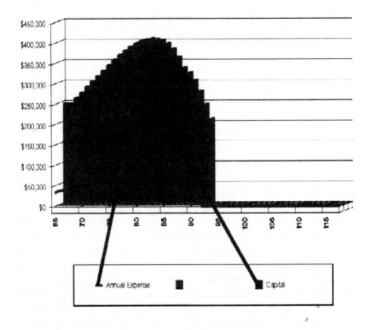

As inflation increases the amount of income needed for your standard of living, there is the potential need to draw increasing amounts out of savings, investments and retirement accounts.

The graph shows how long your capital will last. The objective is to assure that your capital is properly managed so that it will last at least until your life expectancy.

If the capital is depleted before your need for income has ceased, then you will become dependent on your pensions, social security, relatives or public sources. If there is capital remaining when your need for income stops then the remaining capital is available for your heirs.

The line allows you to visualize the annual expenses as compared to your capital accounts.

If the bars dip below the "0" level on the graph, it indicates that you have consumed all your savings, investment and retirement accounts, and your spending requirements have caused a "deficit" spending situation - a need for funds where none exists.

Now, when presented with this set of facts, we had a suggestion for them. Sell their house, and use the home sale tax exemption to shelter all their taxable profit on the sale so they would pay no tax.

Then, we recommended they pay cash for a home in the $170,000 range they had been looking at, putting an additional $71,000 of cash into their investment pool. (They had told us they had found a town home for $170,000 that was brand new, right near all the kids and grandkids, and would make them happy.)

And, because of moving to the smaller home, their monthly expenses would drop about $400, reducing their need to $2,600 a month.

As the next chart and graph show, by reducing their monthly income need and adding money to their investment pool, they would still run out of money at age 85 if they kept earning 3%. (Projection 3)

But, instead of having to earn 12% or more to make their money last as long as they'll probably live, they would only need to earn 6.5% (a much more realistic rate to attain without taking too much risk) to have their assets last until age 99! (Projection 4)

This example is EXACTLY how you have to figure out your ability to make your assets last for your lifetime.

There is no other way than using this type of projection to learn what you should do. Of course, these projections aren't any guarantee of how things will turn out. Inflation could be higher or lower than we projected. Their investment returns could be different than those projected.

Their need for income could end up being different than they thought. All the assumptions we made when planning could end up being different. So, while there is no guarantee of 100% accuracy with any projection about anything in life...

Planning still gives you a "roadmap" to follow.

Planning gives you a way to measure your situation and make changes in a calm, business-like manner... instead of making decisions from fear!

That's why PLANNING is so crucial. It gives you a path to follow based on realistic assumptions. And, as you monitor your plan every year (or more often, if need be), you can adjust and fine tune your moves to keep the plan, and your money, on track!

So, yes, this is the only way we know of to have the absolutely best chance of making sure your money lasts until you don't need it any more! Again, PLANNING is the key!

Retirement Capital Projection: CLARA AND BRYAN PROJECTION 3

Ages		Annual Expenses incl. tax	Less: Earned income	Retirement acct distr.*	Investment acct distr.*	Pensions' Soc Sec	Other income	Annual surp.us	Begin. year Account totals
		1	2	3	4	5	6	7	8
65	64	$31,200				$9,456	$71,000	$49,256	$246,788
66	65	32,448			7,841	24,607			304,925
67	66	33,745			8,874	24,871			305,994
68	67	35,095			9,955	25,140			306,033
69	68	36,576			11,162	25,414			304,956
70	69	37,969		1,979	10,297	25,693			302,608
71	70	39,653		2,031	11,645	25,978			299,040
72	71	41,414		2,083	13,064	26,267			293,923
73	72	44,447		2,137	15,748	26,562			287,137
74	73	46,787		2,192	17,733	26,862			277,327
75	74	48,856		2,248	19,440	27,168			265,121
76	75	50,883		2,305	21,099	27,479			250,732
77	76	52,985		2,352	22,837	27,797			234,147
78	77	55,174		2,410	24,644	28,120			215,225
79	78	57,454		2,457	26,548	28,449			193,815
80	79	59,831		2,504	28,543	28,784			169,752
81	80	62,308		2,550	30,633	29,125			142,864
82	81	64,888		2,596	32,819	29,473			112,969
83	82	67,433		2,641	34,965	29,827			79,879
84	83	66,808		34,704	1,915	30,188		(1)	43,543
85	84	74,406		7,177		30,555		(36,724)	7,127
86	85	71,302				30,929		(40,372)	
87	86	42,658				22,430		(20,227)	
88	87	44,364				15,867		(28,497)	
89	88	46,139				16,134		(33,005)	
90	89	47,985				16,405		(31,579)	
91	90	49,904				15,230		(34,674)	

Note: Cl* = client life expectancy age Sp* = spouse life expectancy age

*Investment and Retirement distributions include withdrawals from account totals to satisfy "Income needed" shortages from Cash Flow report

52

PROJECTION 3

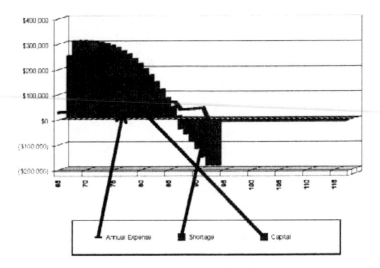

As inflation increases the amount of income needed for your standard of living, there is the potential need to draw increasing amounts out of savings, investments and retirement accounts.

The graph shows how long your capital will last. The objective is to assure that your capital is properly managed so that it will last at least until your life expectancy.

If the capital is depleted before your need for income has ceased, then you will become dependent on your pensions, social security, relatives or public sources. If there is capital remaining when your need for income stops then the remaining capital is available for your heirs.

The line allows you to visualize the annual expenses as compared to your capital accounts.

If the bars dip below the "0" level on the graph, it indicates that you have consumed all your savings, investment and retirement accounts, and your spending requirements have caused a "deficit" spending situation - a need for funds where none exists.

Retirement Capital Projection: CLARA AND BRYAN — PROJECTION 4

Ages		Annual Expenses incl. tax	Earned income	Retirement acct distr.*	Investment acct distr.*	Pensions/ Soc Sec	Other income	Annual surplus	Begin. year Account totals
		1	2	3	4	5	6	7	8
65	64	$31,200				$9,456	$71,000	$49,256	$246,788
66	65	32,448			7,841	24,607			315,287
67	66	34,109			9,238	24,871			327,427
68	67	35,672			10,532	25,140			338,870
69	68	37,425			12,011	25,414			349,677
70	69	39,075		2,339	11,043	25,693			359,612
71	70	40,659		2,482	12,200	25,978			368,733
72	71	42,428		2,633	13,528	26,267			377,062
73	72	44,317		2,792	14,963	26,562			384,358
74	73	46,361		2,961	16,538	26,862			390,430
75	74	48,418		3,140	18,110	27,168			395,039
76	75	50,406		3,329	19,598	27,479			398,082
77	76	52,466		3,512	21,137	27,797			399,539
78	77	54,614		3,722	22,773	28,120			399,233
79	78	56,852		3,923	24,480	28,449			396,964
80	79	59,188		4,133	26,271	28,784			392,515
81	80	61,624		4,353	28,146	29,125			385,646
82	81	64,321		4,582	30,266	29,473			376,099
83	82	67,253		4,820	32,606	29,827			363,431
84	83	70,326		5,067	35,072	30,188			347,194
85	84	73,528		5,287	37,686	30,555			327,012
86	85	76,546		5,510	40,106	30,929			302,500
87	86	48,370		5,737	20,203	22,430			273,578
88	87	46,386		5,966	17,602	22,818			263,731
89	88	47,746		6,195	18,338	23,214			255,772
90	89	49,776		6,366	19,794	23,616			246,267
91	90	51,998		6,528	22,895	22,574			234,412
92	91	54,306		6,680	24,634	22,992			218,310
93	92	56,593		6,818	26,358	23,417			199,149
94	93	59,114		6,862	28,402	23,850			176,760
95	94	61,967		6,883	30,792	24,292			150,692
96	95	64,999		6,878	33,380	24,741			120,361
97	96	68,173		6,676	33,297	25,199			85,308
98	97	65,927		40,263		25,665			45,085
99	98	73,386		5,135		17,635			5,175

Note - CY* = client life expectancy age   Sp* = spouse life expectancy age
*Investment and Retirement distributions include withdrawals from account totals to satisfy "Income needed" shortages from Cash Flow report

PROJECTION 4

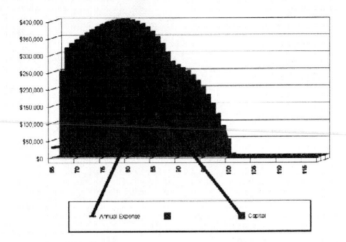

As inflation increases the amount of income needed for your standard of living, there is the potential need to draw increasing amounts out of savings, investments and retirement accounts.

The graph shows how long your capital will last. The objective is to assure that your capital is properly managed so that it will last at least until your life expectancy.

If the capital is depleted before your need for income has ceased, then you will become dependent on your pensions, social security, relatives or public sources. If there is capital remaining when your need for income stops then the remaining capital is available for your heirs.

The line allows you to visualize the annual expenses as compared to your capital accounts.

If the bars dip below the "0" level on the graph, it indicates that you have consumed all your savings, investment and retirement accounts, and your spending requirements have caused a "deficit" spending situation - a need for funds where none exists.

55

Think about it ...

- **It's simply a question of mathematics.**

- **Accumulate your documents and numbers.**

- **Put the numbers into a computer program.**

- **Project the rate of inflation.**

- **Factor in the amount of money you will need per month in both today's dollars and future dollars.**

The projection results will tell you:

> **What rate of return you need to earn on your money, and**
> **How long the money will last under different assumptions.**

PLAN, PLAN, PLAN

Chapter 9

THE BIGGEST MISTAKES RETIREES MAKE AND HOW TO AVOID THEM

ℬ

Over the years, we've spent countless hours working with retirees and pre-retirees. We've seen just about everything.

We've seen people who have wonderful, secure retirements and have done many things right. We've also seen many people who have not-so-wonderful retirements and have done lots of things wrong.

Please understand that this is not criticism. It's not our place to criticize. What we are trying to do is show you how easy it is to get messed up with your retirement planning and point out some of the most common mistakes people make so you won't make them yourself.

Many people wonder how can so many retirees can be in such a fix? If it's such a problem, our country would really be in big trouble with retirees everywhere who were suffering financially. The answer is, it is true, it is a problem --there are many retirees suffering financially, and as the Baby Boom Generation ages, retirees will become this country's largest financial problem of all!

So, with that said, we want to make sure you understand everything you need to know to plan properly for your own retirement. When you finish this book and start your retirement planning, you will be well ahead of your peers.

Now, let's talk about the biggest mistakes retirees make and how to avoid them.

Do you know if your retirement money will really last and provide you the life-style you want?

The only way to be sure is to avoid making any of the ten biggest mistakes people make when they retire!

It's frightening when you think about it, but your retirement doesn't leave too much room for mistakes of any kind.

Right?

It's kind of like building a house. The contractor doesn't have more than an inch or two of room for error. If they're off by more than that, the house may not stand up.

As big as a house is, there exists only the tiniest margin to be off from the plans. And, the same situation occurs with your retirement. Your retirement is not any different than a house. It has to have a foundation. It has to have walls that won't come crashing down around you. It is a thing that you must have working for you, 24 hours a day, seven days a week, 365 days a year, year in and year out!

In other words, your retirement cannot be "built" by the seat of your pants, it must be:

Safe, Secure, And On A Solid Foundation!

Let us share a quick story with you, to illustrate some of the mistakes we mentioned a few minutes ago, and then we'll discuss them in more detail.

Perry sat in a sort of stunned silence. His wife Edie, fidgeted with her purse that was sitting on the edge of the desk of their accountant, Bob.

Bob was struggling to find some words to comfort them, but just didn't seem to be able to find the right ones. He did manage to say, "Well, I know this is a shock, but I promise I'll do everything I can to make it easier for you."

He knew his words rang hollow on Perry and Edie. The silence of a few seconds seemed like an eternity to Bob.

Finally, Perry spoke up. "But Bob, I don't understand how this could be legal. I mean, it's our money. Why don't we have the right to do what we want with it? It seems so unfair!" His voice started to rise in a more angry tone. "Why should we be forced to withdraw money out of our own IRAs when we don't want to? It's our money, not the government's..."

Edie was the next person to speak. "You know Bob, Perry is right. We've worked for all those years, paid all those taxes, raised a family, and, well, it just makes no sense. How can we be penalized for keeping our own money nice and safe in the bank? How can they make us take our own money out and then get stuck paying taxes when we don't need to use the money now?"

Bob tried to answer both of them. He looked down over the top of his glasses and sipped on his Styrofoam cup of coffee. After swallowing his coffee, he answered, "Well, I know that these kind of laws make no sense, but there really isn't anything we can do about it now. If you had been my clients before, I would have told you about this three years ago, and we could have avoided the whole thing. I'm really sorry."

Perry then asked, "What about the bank? Why didn't they tell us? Aren't they required to inform people about this ridiculous penalty? Are all their customers getting nailed the way we are? How were we supposed to know?"

Bob responded. "I don't know what happened, to be honest with you. When I called Carol over at the bank, she said they have a policy of sending out notices to their customers in the year they are turning 70 ½ so they don't forget about this. I guess they never got your change of address entered into their computer or something, and your forwarding notice expired from the post office."

"That's not good enough!" Edie stammered. "It's just not fair. How were we supposed to know....," her voice trailed off in sadness. "Well, Perry. Let's go. It doesn't seem that anything is going to happen to change this. Bob here says that we messed up, and even though we had no knowledge of this stupid law, we're stuck. Is that about the size of it Bob?"

Bob nodded his head in agreement as he sipped his coffee. He put the cup down, grabbed their IRS notices in a pile, and straightened them out by bouncing the bottoms of the paper on the top of his desk. He then asked, "Would you like me to try another letter to the IRS? I will, but I don't think it will make any difference. And, you know that the penalties and interest keep mounting every day until they get the money from you."

Perry stood up and pushed his chair back from the desk. Edie did the same. Perry looked at Edie and said, "I don't think we should waste any more of either Bob's or our time, do you? Let's face it, the longer we wait to pay, the more it's going to cost us. I don't know, we might as well get it over with and write them their dang check!"

Edie closed her purse after putting away her reading glasses. She said, "I guess you're right, honey. If the IRS has nothing better to do than punish 74-year old people, then I guess we're just going to have to live with it."

She then turned to Bob and asked, "How much is the total with all the interest and everything?"

Bob looked at the top sheet in the pile of correspondence and replied, "Well, if we get the check to them by next Tuesday, there won't be any more interest than is already on top of the penalties. The total is $17,657.23." He almost choked on the words as they came out of his mouth.

Then he added, "Plus, we'll have to have you make a withdrawal from both IRAs of, let's see, Perry, you need to withdraw $9,988, and Edie, uh, you have to get $6,567 out of yours."

Bob continued, "Now remember, you'll have to set aside about 35% of these withdrawals to cover the federal and state taxes that will be due next year. You'll also have to make estimated payments on the 15th, and I'll explain how to do that before then."

Perry and Edie picked up their stuff and shook Bob's hand. Perry mumbled some sort of thanks as he and Edie turned to leave the office. As Perry held the door open for Edie, she turned to him and said, "We'll get through this. I know we will."

Perry let the door close behind him and put his arm around Edie as he replied, "I know honey. We will get through this, but I am so mad at that bank..."

Edie cut him off and said, "Perry, it's not the bank's fault. It's ours. We should have known..."

Now it was Perry's turn to cut Edie off. "How the heck were we supposed to know that you have to withdraw certain amounts out of your IRA? Bill, the genius accountant, never told us. The bank never told us. No one told us except the IRS agent!"

Perry stopped talking because he was going over the same angry path he'd been on many times before. A path that let him get his anger out, but didn't change their tax bill a cent.

This sad but true story demonstrates how retirees are constantly at risk to see their retirement security and peace of mind diminish or disappear. The world is a much tougher and unforgiving place than it was years ago. There are so many things to know. So many rules and regulations. So many pitfalls and traps.

Inflation, the tax man and the crazy up and down stock market are always lurking out there, waiting to gobble up more of your estate.

Then there's the kids, or grandchildren, and their demands on your resources.
There's a lot to deal with.

And, let's face it. Who has the time to sit and read every tax law, investment option, insurance issue, and so forth.

And, even if you had the time to read all this stuff, would you really understand what it means? That's why we have included this chapter.

We wanted you to have an easy to understand set of facts, that cut right through all the baloney, and tell you the biggest mistakes retirees make...and more importantly, how to avoid them!

You Need To Know How To Avoid
The Traps That Are Out There!

So let's get into these important issues, and see if you're making any (or all) of these mistakes!

Listening To The Wrong People!

It never ceases to amaze us how many people take advice on their retirement from people who are totally unqualified to give this critical advice!

For example, when we see retirement messes (which we see everyday) and we ask where they got this information that has messed them up so badly, we inevitably hear things like:

"My brother-in-law told me to do that. He used to be an accountant at Westrand Corporation, you know!"

"I asked the guy whose office was next to mine for all these years. I figured he must know what he's doing since he's friends with the boss."

"I read an article by June Brant Queen in _Newstime_ , that said all retirees should do..."

And so on.

Everyone's got an opinion about what you should do with your retirement.

Unfortunately, just because they are your relative or are involved in some area of finance unrelated to retirement planning (like the person at the bank who takes applications for checking accounts and CDs) or write articles for national magazines, doesn't mean they know the answers to YOUR retirement problems and questions.

We cannot stress enough how important it is for you to work with a specialist in retirement planning that knows this area backwards and forwards.

After all, how many times are you going to retire?

Shouldn't you be sure that the advice you're getting is right for you and not generic or just plain wrong?

Be sure to find a retirement specialist just like you would look for a cardiologist if you had a heart problem.

Would you ask your brother-in-law to analyze your angiogram? If not, why would you ask him to analyze your entire financial situation?

It just doesn't make a lot of sense!

2. Choosing The Wrong Pension Option!

Let me illustrate this mistake with a real life example.

The client, Lou, had retired a few years ago from a large equipment manufacturing company. His wife, Janet, had not worked outside the home and had no pension of her own.

When Lou left the company, he was given a range of choices of how to handle his pension payout if he were to die before Janet.

The choices were quite confusing, and they both decided to take the higher payout now, counting on the life insurance Lou had to cover Janet if he died. (With the help of Janet's sister's husband, who used to be an accountant, of course.)

Anyway, Lou died just one year after retirement in a tragic accident. Janet was left with no pension income, but did get Lou's life insurance proceeds.

She Had To Go To Work, Because She Outlived Her Retirement Money!

In a matter of only four years, Janet had to get a job because the amount of life insurance money was way too low for her needs. See, what seemed to be a fortune to them wasn't really a fortune any more.

What did they do wrong?

They made a critical decision like this from the seat of their pants, without having someone prepare a detailed financial projection of which option would best meet their needs, before making the irrevocable election.

If Lou and Janet had done this, she would be receiving a much higher income and have the insurance proceeds to boot.

Now, does this mean that all retirees should take the lower payouts and have the survivor get some sort of payout?

No, not at all. There is no such thing as any strategy that applies to some or all retirees. Your situation is your situation. It is as unique as your fingerprints. And just like no two fingerprints are alike, no two retirements are alike.

Please promise us you'll not take "canned" advice, particularly when it comes to monumental decisions like choosing a retirement payout.

3. Misunderstanding What Medicare And Social Security Do And Don't Pay For!

We see it all the time.

One spouse told us how shocked she was when she learned that the $3,500 a month nursing home expense for her very ill spouse wasn't covered by Medicare or Social Security.

"But I thought Medicare covered medical expenses!" she exclaimed.

The Government Is Not Going
To Take Care Of You!

Yes, Medicare does cover medical expenses. But, it only covers certain ones, and only after you have paid a deductible.

Many, many medical expenses aren't covered by Medicare and are usually picked up by a Medicare Supplement policy. But, those supplements still don't cover extended nursing home care.
Not a penny. Zilch. (Except for up to 100 days of skilled care which very few retirees get because of all the red tape. But, even if you DO get this 100 day Medicare payment, what happens to you on day 101?)

Here again, we have an unplanned-for situation that can literally wipe out a family's retirement nest egg; a situation that nine out of ten retirees don't have a clue about!

(By the way, as we've discussed elsewhere, did you know that in order to qualify for state support from Medicaid, you literally have to spend your net worth down to nearly zero first? This is not a solution that we recommend you implement!)

Don't make the mistake of thinking that Medicare or Social Security is going to take care of you. They don't! Sure, they cover many things, but there are still huge, gigantic gaps they won't take care of if you don't plan for yourself. You must know what the government does help you with and what they don't help you with. And, you must have a plan to address the exposed areas that could cause your family some real problems!

4. Not Understanding The Tax Rules For
IRAs. Pensions. Income. Etc.!

Remember our friends, Perry and Edie, who found out too late that the IRS demands you remove certain amounts out of your IRA? Remember how devastated they were with all the penalties and interest they got stuck with? And, remember how aggravated they were that no one told them about it, yet they still got stung big time?

Well, their story is just one of many problems that retirees run into because of a lack of the proper knowledge about qualified retirement plans.

63

"Uncle Sam" Is A Relative You Should
Try To Give As Little As Possible To!

How much should you withdraw from the plans? When should you withdraw from the plans? Should you let that money sit, use other money to live off and pay bills?

Or, should you take a withdrawal from your IRA to pay off your car so you'll have lower monthly payments?

Or, how should your beneficiaries be named in order to minimize their taxes in light of IRS regulations?

Or, should you stop working at a certain time to collect Social Security now?

Or, should you wait to apply?

Or, should you work part time? And, how does that affect your Social Security payments?

What about the taxes on your Social Security income? Are there legal and safe ways to reduce it?

Or, what about the taxes on the interest on your CDs? Is there a better way to invest to reduce those taxes?

Or,..........We think you get our point.

There are literally dozens and dozens of tax decisions you must make, whether you want to deal with them or not.

Let's think about a simple example here. If you were to save $200 a month in taxes, simply by knowing the laws and how to legally reduce your taxes, that's $2,400 a year that you didn't have before.

What could you do with an extra $2,400?

What about saving even more? People do it all the time.

Could You Use A Few Hundred
Dollars Extra Each Month?

If you want to make sure your income, estate and gift taxes are as low as legally possible, you need to work with a qualified financial professional who can lay out all your options for you, allowing you to make an informed decision as opposed to an emotional decision.

Or worse, not even knowing you had to make a decision, like Perry and Edie who found out the hard way.

Now, you may be thinking, well, I know about the required withdrawals and all that. And that's fine.

But, what does someone else know that you don't know?

When it comes to tax planning, there is little room for making mistakes. Don't try to know it all yourself or depend on others who don't study these things every single day for a living!

(Did you know that each and every year, there are hundreds of tax rule changes? Some of them don't affect you and others do!)

So don't play tax roulette and hope your numbers hit. Make sure you are as sensible about your tax planning as you are about your health!

5. Not Knowing How Inflation Destroys Your Money. And Not Taking Actions To Prevent It From Leaving You Broke!

While we won't repeat the whole inflation discussion here, because we've covered it in great detail in other chapters, we still have to add it to the list of the biggest mistakes retirees make.

6. Thinking "Risk" Just Involves Losing Principal!

Here is a big mistake we deal with almost every day and have covered in the chapter on investments. We're repeating it here since it is so critical to your wealth.

A client that's either planning for, or already is, retired, will say something like, "We don't want to take any `risk' with our retirement funds! We want them to be totally safe and free of risk'!"

(Have you ever thought that yourself?)

There's More Risk In "Riskless" Investments Than You May Think!

Let's discuss what the definition of "risk" is, in the first place. If you look it up in the dictionary, you'll see that it is defined as: "A chance of encountering a loss or harm, a hazard or danger."

Now, you'll notice it doesn't say "loss of principal." It is defined as "loss."

This is a major distinction we need to make here.

Most retirees think "risk" means that you put your investments somewhere and the $100,000 you started with is now worth far less than$ 100,000. And yes, this is one type of risk...and a real one at that!

But it is only one type of risk. There are others that are just as scary and that can hurt you just as badly as losing principal.

By the way, if we told you that you are actually losing real money in the bank, would you believe us? Would you think we were lying, because CDs are insured by the FDIC? We guess this is the time to explain what we mean.

If you are making 3% interest on a CD, and you are in the 25% tax bracket, your net, after-tax yield is only 2.25%!

$$
\begin{array}{r}
\text{A 3.00\% yield} \\
\text{x 25\% tax} = \quad .75\% \text{ lost to taxes} \\
\hline
2.25\% \text{ net after-tax yield.}
\end{array}
$$

Now, that would be bad enough, but we cannot forget our nemesis, inflation.

Yes, they claim inflation has been licked. That it's gone. Why? Because it's been hovering around 3% for the last couple of years. And that is considered low by today's standards.

But, did you know that in the early `70's, when President Nixon instituted price controls, inflation was an incredibly high 4%!

Isn't that interesting?

In 1972, 4% inflation was considered so high that the government tried putting price controls in place. Now, when inflation is at the same exact level 30 years later, it's considered insignificant.

How can this be? Could it be that inflation has changed, or is it possible that the government has changed the way they want us to view it?

How does this "not so bad" inflation affect our CD?

Losing Money On Riskless Investments Is Very Real!

Well, remember that we're at 2.25% net, after-tax yield. Now let's subtract inflation from this yield to arrive at your true change in value, adjusted for the loss of purchasing power:

2.25% net, after-tax yield
- 3.00% inflation
(0.75%) True return

Those brackets, by the way, mean a **negative real rate of return!**

Yes, that means that you have a loss of value of $75 for each $10,000 you have invested in CDs in our example.

Now, if we asked you to put money in an investment that was guaranteed to lose $75 for each $10,000 you invested, you'd run away faster than a deer from a lion. Yet, if you have CDs, then you could be doing the exact same thing!

So, what does a retiree do to get a better return and avoid the higher tax on their Social Security and other income?

As we said a couple of minutes ago, the real secret is to know what items you can invest in that are off of the "tax hit list."

What you need to do is figure out how much monthly income you need, and then build a plan that uses the tax favored savings to assure you get the cash flow you need, and avoid wasting money on the taxes you don't need, with assets that have some chance to keep up with inflation.

See, the risk we're talking about here is the risk of losing purchasing power.

This risk is so profound, yet almost totally ignored by most retirees. That is until it's too late!

The only way to insure you won't run out of money is to have a plan that both meets your income needs and provides the opportunity to keep up with inflation.

Now, no one is suggesting you not keep a portion of your money in CDs or other guaranteed programs, because it would be foolish not to.

But, by the same token, having too much money in these types of investments can insure you have a high risk of running out of money!

No one wants to outlive their money.

Misunderstanding the risk of the loss of purchasing power is a mistake you do not want to make.

7. Paying For The Wrong Kinds
And Wrong Amounts Of Insurance!

For some reason, when people are retired, many of them hang on to old insurance coverage of all types, just because they've had them for a long time and are reluctant to change.

We're not sure why, but it seems to be the case more often than not.

Listen, when you are in retirement, you have little extra room in your budget to waste money on needless coverage, or to be shortchanging yourself on coverage you do need. Many of our retired clients find they can get more coverage in the areas they do need and eliminate or reduce coverage on stuff they don't need and save hundreds or thousands of dollars in the process!

We recently saw a couple in their late 60's, who were paying over $2,100 a year for coverage they didn't need, and had no insurance at all on things that they really should have in place.

By repositioning their insurance portfolio, we showed them how to buy what they needed at less cost.

The net bottom line is that they have an excellent group of coverage for just about anything that could go wrong and can save $123 a month to spend and have fun!

No one wants you to be insurance poor, and we also don't want you wasting money on things you truly don't need, either!

The only answer is to have someone objectively review your insurance and find out what's wrong and what's right!

8. Planning For Your Retirement
When You Are Already Retired!

This mistake is one that we see over and over again.

People getting laid off from a job they've had for years. Or taking advantage of an early retirement program offered by companies trying to shrink their payrolls.

Or, people taking normal retirement at age 65.

Or, whatever reason.

We have people coming in constantly asking the same question:

68

"Will we have enough money to make it all the way with the same lifestyle?"

This is a big mistake! Why?

Because they have already made all their decisions.

They have already taken their retirement plans and either had them distributed, or are receiving monthly payouts. They have made all their choices, and want us to tell them they're going to be OK.

In some cases they will be. And in some cases they won't if they continue on their original path. Of course, things may seem alright now, but they haven't peered down the road twenty years to see the consequences of their decisions.

If we're making any sense to you, you'll see that waiting until you reach a certain age to plan for that same age usually doesn't work.

We have folks that came to us under these circumstances, and we have the unpleasant job of telling them unless they modify their current plans, they will be out of money somewhere down the road.

Their response, occasionally, is to fire us because we brought them the bad news. (They chopped off the head of the messenger!)

They were going to find themselves in the same position as Grandma Hannah.

So, if you're not yet retired, do some detailed planning right NOW! Don't wait until you are retired to start.

Now, if you have already retired, it's never too late to start planning. Which brings us to the most important mistake of all to avoid:

9. Not Doing Consistent, Careful Ongoing Planning!

Yes, planning is the single, most effective technique to have a safe and secure retirement!

The reason most of us aren't going to win the retirement game is that we don't follow this crucial sequence when it comes to managing our finances:

- Figure out where you are today.
- Figure out where you want to be.
- Get a true understanding of the options you have available to you. (Not from biased sources.)
- Develop a plan that will provide the right" course" to follow.

- Make the changes necessary to get the plan going.
- Monitor your progress, and make the proper adjustments to keep the plan "on course."

So keep these mistakes in mind as you think about your retirement, your security, and your peace of mind! We want you to be aware of the fact that making mistakes in some things aren't so bad, because you have time to recover. If you're 35, and make a mistake with investing, you have plenty of time to regroup. If you're 75, the same mistake can be deadly

As we said before, you only retire once. (In most cases.) So, you have to be very, very careful...and plan, plan, plan!

Think about it.

The biggest mistakes retirees make are:

- **Listening to the wrong people.**

- **Choosing the wrong pension option.**

- **Misunderstanding what Medicare and Social Security do and do not pay for.**

- **Not understanding the tax rules for IRAs, pensions, 401(k)s, etc.**

- **Not knowing how inflation destroys your money, and not taking actions to prevent it from leaving you broke.**

- **Thinking "risk" just involves losing principal.**

- **Paying for the wrong kinds and wrong amounts of insurance.**

- **Planning for your retirement when you are already retired.**

- **Not doing consistent, careful, ongoing planning.**

Chapter 10

HOW TO PROTECT YOUR ASSETS FROM BEING TAKEN AWAY IF YOU OR A LOVED ONE NEEDS LONG-TERM MEDICAL CARE!

೮೦

As sad as it may be, here's a dose of reality for you: If you or a loved one find yourselves in need of long term medical care, the government will do all that it can to first have YOU pay every single dime that you can, out of YOUR pocket, before they step into "help."

If you're like most average Americans, you probably think you've done a pretty good job at socking away some cash for emergency use or to have fun with when you retire.

Now, upon reading this book, you may have realized some mistakes you've made in planning your financial future. That's okay. Chances are you can still make some changes and achieve a better outcome. But you need to dispel some myths.

One of the biggest myths among retirees is...'I've got a few investments stashed away in case of an emergency...We'll be just fine if anything suddenly comes up!"

Short of begging you to please alter this misconception right away, let's share an example of what happened to one family.

Judy's husband was an alcoholic. After getting fired from his executive position he had held for close to thirty years, Glen had to be checked into a care facility. He was only three years away from retirement.

We'll make a long and heart-wrenching story short. Glen had more than a problem with alcohol -- he also underwent heart surgery, was being treated for diabetes, given daily enzymes for his liver condition, and treated for severe depression. (As horrifying as it was to his wife and family, they felt helpless and couldn't do a darn thing as this once strong and vibrant man diminished in front of their eyes.)

His devastating health condition wasn't the only problem Judy's family faced. She also had bills piling so high, they could be stacked to the moon and back. She couldn't figure out how to pay the astronomical medical expenses.

See, Glen had been fired, so there went their chances of collecting his full pension and other benefits. However, up to this point they still had medical insurance to cover his expenses for awhile.

Throughout the years, they thought they had been really smart and put aside a bit of money in their savings account. They had a few CDs, their IRAs and a few other minor investments.

But as fate would have it, these finances were wiped out.

Now reality hit them hard.

They Never Thought They'd Need Long-Term Care!

Just like so many other folks out there, they thought they were immune from needing long-term care. And since they wrongfully believed it "only happened to other people," they neglected to calculate the long-term care risk into their retirement planning!

Glen had to be admitted permanently into a nursing home after his many lengthy stays at various hospitals and treatment centers. His body had gone into shock from all the surgeries, medications, and the overall effects of "drying out" from alcohol.

Four years later, Glen passed away. Their funds had been completely exhausted from paying the long-term care expenses. Judy even had to take out a loan from her sister to pay for Glen's funeral.

So let's take a look at how their plan of just "stashing away" some money failed them.

When Judy was fighting her battle with the medical bills, she tried what she thought was every avenue of getting some financial help. And she was consistently denied.

Believe it or not (and you had better believe it!), government aid was denied because Judy and Glen did not seem "needy!"

The government's calculations of their CDs, IRAs, their home, Judy's 401 (k), and the other miscellaneous investments disqualified them for government financial assistance. The ONLY fortunate thing in their situation was that Glen was a retired Veteran. This gave them a small amount of financial help, but that was it.

While many medical bills were covered by health insurance, others weren't, and Judy had to begin the process of cleaning out all of their savings, assets and investments. Then, when Glen went into the nursing home, Judy discovered that only the first 100 days of Glen's care were covered by Medicare, and only the actual medical expenses. The costs associated with custodial care weren't covered at all.

Medicaid didn't kick in until Judy had gone through a large portion of their retirement nest egg. She was allowed to keep some equity in her house, but nearly everything else was wiped out. She eventually had to sell the house and give half the proceeds to Medicaid anyway! (Every state has its own rules on what a spouse can retain.)

With the half that was left, she bought a small condo and had to rely on her kids for financial help. By the time this ordeal was over, and because Judy and Glen hadn't thought of "protecting their assets," Judy was left with virtually NOTHING!

You DON'T Have To Let This Happen To YOU!

You, just like Glen and Judy, have the opportunity to make financial decisions to help prevent this. You have the opportunity to make sure you don't lose everything to pay for long-term care.

The risk of long-term care is a reality for everyone. No one is special or immune from falling ill and requiring long- term care.

We understand that most people don't like to think about this (remember how upsetting it was to write up your will?).

Most of us like to pretend that we'll live forever and prefer not to think of doom and gloom. And to be honest, we wish we could really live in that dream world, too!

But the harsh reality is that it can happen. In fact, government statistics say that once we reach age 65, we have a 43% chance of going into a nursing home sometime during our lives. And since the average American loses most of their assets if they go into a nursing home, that may mean you have a 43% chance of losing everything you've got. So, you have to be prepared.

You don't have to be like Judy and Glen and watch your hard work and earnings disappear practically overnight. If you want to be a smart planner and skillfully prepare for your retirement (which we assume, since you're reading this book), then you also have to

Plan In Order To Keep Your Hard-Earned Assets...

Just remember the two aspects of planning:

1) Plan and structure your financial portfolio for a secure and peaceful retirement; and,
2) Plan and structure your financial portfolio to be protected from catastrophic and unforeseen expenses.

These two points are the foundation and essence of any sound retirement plan.

The last thing we want to see happen to you is to take the first step in planning your retirement so that it is secure and peaceful, and then lose it all because you failed to take the second step to protect yourself.

See, if you fail to plan the latter, you'll end up like Judy. She didn't seek the help to make the right decisions and failed at the most critical part of it all...protecting what she had socked away from being taken to pay for the enormous long-term care expenses.

If your assets are just sitting there, without a coat of armor around them to shield them ...you are vulnerable.

Your assets are like sitting ducks waiting to be blown out of the water before you know what happened!

We hope you are getting the picture here about how important it is to not only plan your retirement skillfully and intelligently, but also to protect it once you've done the planning.

The last thing we want to do in this book is get statistically dry and boring...so please bear with us through this next section.

There's some important data and information out there that anyone and everyone who ever plans on retiring should know! (We'll try our best to keep it interesting.)

Do you know the answers to these questions?

1. Why should we worry about nursing homes?

First of all, according to The New England Journal of Medicine... Of people who recently turned 65 years of age, 43% will enter a nursing home before they die.. More than half of those people will spend at least a year there, and almost a quarter will spend at least five years of their lives there.

Now, do you think it's valid for us to worry about nursing homes since nearly half of us will end up in one? We think so! And, do you think since the cost of nursing homes is rising at 9.8% every year, that we should be concerned? You bet!

And, at the time we are writing this book, it costs an average of $5,000-8,000 per month for nursing home expenses. Where will this money come from?

Another very good reason to worry about nursing homes and their attached expenses is that life expectancies continue to increase with only modest adjustments to Social Security, while Medicare or other benefits that help support the aged are being reduced.

In fact, instead of increasing the help our elderly desperately need most of these benefits are being cut back.

Let's enlighten you on how our health care system has become so screwed up.

Decades ago, our government planned for such things as health care costs. Great, but back then, the average age for retirement was 65, with an average life expectancy of only 62 years.

Yes, the government is sometimes smarter than we give them credit for.

This was a pretty neat little trick, wouldn't you say? The government collected all sorts of Social Security and Medicare dollars from us --dollars headed for a fund that didn't need to be used! They were covered -- we passed away before we could take advantage of their "plan!" (On average, of course, not everyone died at 62, but the government works on averages.)

We've come a long, long way in terms of health care since this system was first established.

And, in turn, here's what's happened. Today people are living longer, retiring earlier, inflation is constantly on the rise -- tapping into and wiping out the barely existent funds supposedly set aside for us!

We're depending on a source of revenue that simply is not readily available for us to use. The government, for years and years, has collected tax dollars from us to go into these funds. But, did those dollars really go into that fund? Not a chance. As soon as it went in, it went out.

We've paid for all sorts of things, but certainly not our financial futures. Many of the government programs are running at a deficit.

The nice little nest egg funded from our tax dollars and designed to be there when we hit retirement... IS NOT THERE!

Now, in the near future we're at the brink of Social Security and Medicare going bankrupt. This leads us to our next question...

2. Who in the heck pays for nursing homes if the government hasn't appropriately set up the health care system and funds to help us out?

You now probably know the answer to this one... YOU DO!

You and you alone will be responsible for paying for long-term care nursing home expenses.

While the government doesn't want to talk about it, it requires people lose almost everything they have before kicking in with Medicaid payments.

You CAN lose some or ALL of the equity in your home! You CAN be forced to sign over your Social Security checks and pension checks to the state!

You can be forced to sell your property, everything you spent your whole life working for!

Already over 40% of all nursing home and medical bills are paid by individuals.

Are you prepared to pay $7,000 a month today, or the expected $12,000 a month it will cost in less than a decade?

If you're like most Americans... the answer is "No!"

It doesn't matter if you're rich and famous or living off a low fixed income, we don't know many people who can easily drop thousands of dollars each month into nursing home expenditures.

Even if you had loads of money, wouldn't you rather see it earn a large return for you to enjoy or pass on to your heirs?

So, since chances are you'd rather come up with a better way to pay for long-term care rather than having your own assets wiped out, let's examine Medicaid and its uses.

The first thing to always remember is that Medicaid will NOT help you out with nursing home expenses until you run almost completely out of money.

That means, all your sources of income must be exhausted (that means anything you own including your car, home, pension plans, investments and so forth) before Medicaid will kick in to help you.

Do you see the importance here? To make sure this point doesn't slip by, here it is again:

More than likely... you will not be eligible for any of the government's financial assistance programs for nursing (that you've been paying for all of your working life) home care until most or all of your assets are wiped out!

There, we hope that hit home!

So, to answer our initial question of who pays for nursing home costs...the answer is YOU. Medicare does NOT pay the bill, as most people think. In the real world, Medicare covers very little of America's nursing home bills.

Let's repeat.

MEDICARE COVERS VERY LITTLE OF AMERICA'S NURSING HOME BILLS!

It's shocking, as well as upsetting, to know that most people mistakenly believe that Medicare will pay the entire amount. But, this has never been the case, and it will NEVER be the case (unless some magic wand is waved over our health care system -- which is totally unrealistic).

In the best situation, Medicare will only pay the first 100 days of a nursing home stay. But in many situations, it won't even pay that.

And, Medicaid only kicks in when you are BROKE, and your assets are depleted!

In fact, did you know that in most states you won't qualify for Medicaid until you own less than $2,000? So, you have to be almost completely wiped out before you're even considered eligible.

IRAs, pensions, and insurance - no asset is totally exempt.

So here's the deal: If you are incredibly fortunate, you may have a 100-day window of opportunity for Medicare to help pay the costs. But what are you supposed to do after the 100 days is up?

The government doesn't care what you do, as long as you pay. That means you may have to close out every account, wipe out any savings, and cash out all of your investments to help cover the bills.

We know this is difficult for some of you to handle; the thought is very upsetting. Either we have to hope some magic cure is cooked up during the first 100 days to make yourself or your loved one miraculously better. Or, after the 100 days, you have to start selling nearly everything you own.

This is extremely important since the average nursing home stay is about 2.5 years.

It isn't until you are left with less than $2,000 to your name before most government assistance becomes available!

We apologize for being blunt, but we must be realistic.

The good news is that you can do something about it!

Even though we are educating you with the not-so-pretty facts, please keep in mind that you can save yourself from most, if not all this trauma that many people face! It all boils down to proper planning and bullet-proofing your assets from being pulled out from under you. Remember it's not until you are flat broke that you are eligible for assistance!

So, don't put this off!

If you delay, waiting for the "right time," you'll miss your narrow window of opportunity that's awaiting you right now. You must protect your assets and estate properly, right now while you can!

3. What exactly is Medicaid?

If you look up the word "Medicaid" in the dictionary, Webster defines it as "a federal and state program of medical insurance for persons with very low incomes."

And the definition of "Medicare", according to Webster is "a government program of medical insurance for aged or disabled persons."

Simply put, Medicaid is a government-funded program that will pay for your long-term care expenses in a nursing home -- after you are broke.

Currently, Medicaid is a federal program administered by the state. The federal rules apply, or the state will lose its funding. We expect this to change, however. We think the states will end up with "block grants" which is a chunk of money paid to each state, with the state determining how the money will be spent. The state will have control over who gets Medicaid, how much they get, and so on.

The government has simply not updated the Medicaid health care system appropriately since its origin and it is seriously outdated for today's times.

Because the government failed to update the original health care system and make changes to it as the populous changed, we are now facing bankrupt health care funds!

It doesn't take a brain surgeon to figure out why our headlines are screaming out to us, practically daily, about our under-funded health care plans.

Everyone knows that the government programs are losing money, but most politicians are afraid of changing it. None of them want to be the one known as the one who killed Social Security; that doesn't go over very well at re-election time. And now that we are living longer and retiring earlier, we are wiping out an antiquated system that can't handle the demand!

Do yourself a favor and wipe out the notion of this "help for the elderly and disabled" from your mind as if it never existed! That way, you'll be forced to do some of your OWN planning to cover your medical and nursing home expenses in your retirement years.

You have to take the bull by the horns and set yourself up to be financially self-sufficient and reliant. Believe us, you'll be far better off than if you continue to believe in the myth that Medicare and Medicaid will be there to help you out when you need it!

The bottom line is this: Plan your own financial future with a cushion to absorb nursing home costs, because YOU'LL be responsible for paying them. And, while you're at it, be sure to legally, skillfully and creatively protect your assets from being used to pay for these expenses.

Remember, if you're single and have anything above $2,000 to your name, the government won't help you out!

Ask the right questions, seek professional help and you can make the right decisions! Planning is the only sure way to take care of yourself and your family, regardless of what goes on with the health care mess.

4. What are your planning options?

Well, under the new laws, you really only have very limited options to pay for nursing home expenses:

- Use your own assets. You can use your cash, stocks, IRA's, home, etc., to pay for a nursing home stay.

- Transfer assets out of your estate more than 3 to 5 years before anyone applies for Medicaid.

WARNING!

**RECENT CHANGES IN THE LAWS
MAY CAUSE SOME TRANSFERS
TO HAVE ADDITIONAL LEGAL CONSEQUENCES
BEYOND ESTATE OR MEDICAID PLANNING.**

**ANY STRATEGY OF TRANSFERRING ASSETS
INTO FAMILY MEMBERS' NAMES
OR SIMILAR APPROACHES
SHOULD NOT BE DONE WITHOUT FIRST SEEKING PROPER
PLANNING AND LEGAL ADVICE.**

**DO NOT EVEN THINK OF PUTTING A RELATIVE'S NAME ON A
CHECKING ACCOUNT OR CD, GIFTING TO RELATIVES FOR**

COLLEGE EXPENSES, OR OTHER PERSONAL NEEDS WITHOUT PROFESSIONAL ASSISTANCE!

THIS IS NO AREA FOR AMATEUR NIGHT!

- Buy Long Term Care Insurance.

This option may prove to be the best for many of you. You buy enough insurance to cover the risk of going into a nursing home, just like you buy auto insurance to cover the risk of getting into an accident.

Even if you eventually decide to take a pass, and risk paying for a nursing home yourself, possibly wiping out your entire net worth, YOU SHOULD AT LEAST INVESTIGATE THE DIFFERENT KIND OF POLICIES AVAILABLE TO YOU before making a decision!

How can you know if you are comfortable bearing the risk of being wiped out with nursing home expenses without checking out the options that this form of insurance can provide?

You really have to see what choices you have before making any final decisions.

Many retirees automatically assume that they can't afford long-term care insurance. But, unless you've taken the small effort required to see what's available...how can you know?

Don't make assumptions about an area of your financial life that changes all the time, and that is so dangerous! We cannot stress enough that this risk is real and can be fatal to your financial well being.

Let's take a quick look at an example of how this risk of having a nursing home stay can be minimized and how you can protect what you have.

Elaine is 77 and lost her husband, Jack, to a heart attack two years ago. She is in pretty good health, other than a touch of arthritis and some high blood pressure. Jack and Elaine saved quite a bit for themselves over the years, and their assets look like this:

Paid-for home	$150,000
IRAs (now in Elaine's name)	65,000
Stocks and mutual funds	75,000
Life insurance (cash value)	25,000
Bank accounts and CDs	60,000
TOTAL:	$375,000

Now, to a lot of people, this may seem like a lot of money and Elaine will never have to worry about any bills. After all, she's getting $950 month in Social Security and she hardly has any bills to, pay...yet.

Unfortunately, Elaine started getting Alzheimer's disease, and coupled with a mild stroke, she had to have someone come into her home to help take care of her. This home health care was pretty expensive.

For the home health care attendants to take care of her for 8 hours a day, it cost $2,500 per month. Unfortunately, this amount is not covered by most medical insurance or Medicare.

Therefore, she had to take $1,550 out of her savings each month to pay the difference. With the $2,500 a month bill plus the cost of keeping the home, Elaine spends around $3,000 a month, or $36,000 a year. She loses several thousand each year but she still has some money left.

A year went by and Elaine's situation got a bit worse. Her health had deteriorated, and she now has to go into a nursing home for round-the-clock coverage. A halfway decent nursing home in Elaine's community costs $5,000 per month.

With the cost of keeping her house, Elaine realized she'd have to sell the house, especially since she wouldn't be going back. With $3,000 a month, or $36,000 a year, coming out of her savings, Elaine will probably be broke in around ten years or sooner if nursing home costs go up as predicted.

If nursing home costs go up, as they have in the past, Elaine may soon be paying $6,000-7,000 in monthly nursing home costs. At that amount, Elaine will be broke in five years.

In some parts of the country, especially on the east coast, it is not unusual to see monthly nursing home costs between $5,000-9,000 per month. At an annual cost of $60,000-108,000 per year, how long would your assets last?

The bottom line is this: You have only three basic options available to you in order to avoid your family paying for nursing home costs:

1) **Gifting and making asset transfers more than a few years before getting sick, or**
2) **Buying insurance that pays some or all of long-term care expenses, both in and out of a nursing home, or**
3) **Paying for all of it yourself.**

Remember, new laws now make gifting assets more complicated and potentially trouble-causing.

A gifting strategy must be considered very carefully before taking any action! So, insurance may be an option to look at very closely before you rule it out.

If you don't use option one or two, option three is yours by default!

Think about it...

- **Government statistics say that once we reach age 65, we have a 43% chance of going into a nursing home sometime during our lives.**

- **Structure your financial portfolio skillfully and intelligently for a secure and peaceful retirement.**

- **Nursing home expenses and other attached expenses continue to increase without any adjustments made to Social Security, Medicare or other benefits that will help support the aged.**

- **You and you alone will be responsible for paying for long-term care -- nursing home expenses!**

- **You will not be eligible to receive any of the government's financial assistance programs (that you paid for all of your working life) until most or all of your assets are completely cashed out and used for any nursing home costs you incur.**

- **Medicare is defined as "a U.S. government program of medical insurance for aged or disabled persons."**

- **Medicaid is defined as "a federal and state program of medical insurance for persons with low income."**

You have only three options to pay for nursing home expenses:

1) **Pay them yourself dollar-for-dollar.**

2) **Transfer your assets three to five years before you apply for Medicaid.**

3) **Transfer the risk to an insurance company by getting Long Term Care Insurance.**

Chapter 11

HOW TO PROTECT YOUR ASSETS AND YOUR FAMILY WHEN YOU PASS AWAY!

⅋

From dealing with so many clients, we understand that this topic is a difficult one for most people to confront. That's because it reminds us of our own mortality.

In fact, most people prefer to do nothing to secure their families financial future for after they die...simply because they don't like facing the inevitability of death.

You can't turn the other cheek when it comes to planning your finances for when you pass away. If you do, you'll deny your family and loved ones what you want to give them and end up handing over your assets to the IRS and the attorneys!

Like many others, you can continue making excuses and putting off this unpleasant task. It's an easy thing to avoid, because we just don't like facing it.

But, if you neglect to do any estate planning prior to passing away, the IRS and attorneys will jump in to handle your estate. The results could deprive your family and loved ones of the assets that you took a lifetime to accumulate.

The good news is...

You can legally keep the IRS and the attorneys out of your pocket and control exactly who gets what from you!

How would you feel if you worked all of your life and made some good financial investments and decisions in the hope that one day you would be able to pass some of your good fortune onto your heirs...only to never have this happen? And, as a result, create a great big hassle for your loved ones?

Unfortunately, this scenario happens to many good people, because they put off estate planning until it was too late.

When we meet with clients, we find some people at least have Wills written up. Good. Now, the next step is to update that Will (or Will(s) if you have a separate one for your spouse). Things change all the time in people's lives that cause the need to update the Wills and other financial instruments.

For instance, they move. Or they get divorced. Or they get married. Or they pass away. Or they get transferred. Or they lose their job. Or they have children. Or grand-children. Or they retire. Or they buy a second home, or retirement property. And so on.

ALL OF THESE ARE HUGE
FINANCIAL CHANGES IN A PERSON'S LIFE.

Many people don't see how any personal transaction or decision in their lives affects their overall financial lives as well. And because of this oversight, they stand to lose what they've earned.

Sure, you may realize that you need to change or update your Will for certain reasons... but have you? When was the last time you reviewed your Will to make sure everything was up to date? More importantly, do you know if all you need is a Will? For many people a Will alone will not achieve their estate planning goals.

Whatever you do, we hope you don't have to experience a near tragic or a fatal incident in your life to encourage you to sit down with your estate planning attorney and advisors. Make a vow to do it now, and then you will have peace and security no matter what may happen.

And before we move into estate planning in detail, let's promise to at least take the first step in getting you out of the group of people who don't have Wills. If you fall into this category, there's no other option available other than to just do it. If you don't, for many of you, you're asking for trouble.

Because, if you don't have a Will, the government decides how your assets get dispersed. So, don't let this happen to you!

Now, estate planning goes much further than having just a Will. It involves the ownership of your assets, how you have them set up, and how they'll be dispersed. We'll get into Wills, Living Trusts and so forth in just a bit. But remember that most simple Wills don't minimize estate taxes or avoid costly and lengthy probate, and so on.

So, how can you minimize estate taxes? It depends on how you own your assets, and in whose name your assets are held! As we said, the most popular route is for husbands and wives to hold assets jointly, but this may not necessarily be in your best interest.

There's a lot of ways to own your assets and many alternatives to help you avoid losing everything you own and wish to pass on to your loved ones.

Jointly held assets means, if you both own your home, your cars, your bank accounts, investments, etc., and when one of you passes away, you will avoid probate and all the assets will quickly go to the surviving spouse.

And if you own them with right of survivorship, that means 100% of the property or assets goes to the surviving spouse, while again avoiding probate.

So, titling your assets in joint tenancy seems pretty good, right? And it's easy, right? However, it may not be the best way to go! Here are just a few reasons why.

1) **Jointly held assets can be swiped away if there's a dispute, separation, divorce, etc. Or, if you are involved in a lawsuit, even if it only involves one of you.**

2) **Jointly held assets can cause you to lose some control, while you're alive, if they are frozen by the other joint tenant. Or, by the courts, if one or both of you become disabled.**

3) **Jointly held assets minimize all the tax-saving opportunities that are available.**

As important as the first two reasons are, let's focus on the third one for a minute because we're talking mostly about getting you the most in tax-saving advantages! (We'll discuss lawsuits and what you can do in a later chapter.)

First of all, grab a calculator. Seeing as some people think estate planning is only for the wealthy... let's reverse this myth. Add up the value of your house, your cars, your insurance policies (the death benefit), your investments, your savings accounts, your pension plans, any other real estate, any stocks, bonds, jewelry, furniture, stamp collection, etc. See how quickly your assets add up.

If you own anything, it's an asset. For instance, life insurance is not estate tax-free. You may have a $5 million policy and find out you owe the IRS 35% of the death benefit if you own the policy. No, you didn't hear wrong. Life insurance is subject to estate taxes. It is free of income taxes to the beneficiaries, but you have to pay the estate taxes first. Most people don't know that.

Now, either during your lifetime or at your death, you can get away with giving $5 million to your heirs without being penalized with federal estate and/or gift taxes, although in some states you may be hit with an inheritance tax for amounts much less than $5 million.

If you're married, you're not constrained with any predetermined amounts. It's unlimited as to how much you can pass on to your spouse when you pass away, even on top of the $5 million you may have passed on to others.

85

Seems pretty good, right?

Well, let's take a look at what a difference it would make if you were holding these assets in joint tenancy.

Let's say you predecease your spouse who is the joint tenant of your assets. Even though all of your assets would go to the surviving spouse, when that spouse passes away, it's back down to only passing on the $5 million! (Or whatever the new maximum is in the year a death occurs.)

Do you know what this means?

Huge Amounts Of Estate Tax Being Zapped On Your Heirs!

If your assets total more than $5 million, anything above this amount is a target for the state and/or federal government! Your heirs could end up paying anywhere up to 50% of this amount, just in taxes!

See, in this above example, when the first spouse of the jointly held assets passed away, they lost the maximum exemption. This couple could have passed $5 million+ tax-free to other heirs, while having all the rest go tax-free to the surviving spouse!

But they didn't. Because everything was owned jointly, everything went directly to the surviving spouse. And yes, it was tax-free at that time; however, when the surviving spouse passed away, any amount of their jointly held assets over $5 million was taxed!

If they had an estate of $5,500,000, they would needlessly pay tax on $500,000, which would cost the family almost $175,000! $175 grand lost by having their assets in joint tenancy!

Make sense? If you want to save your heirs thousands in tax dollars, then you may want to reconsider owning your assets in joint tenancy.

And, when the surviving spouse passes away, the maximum is $5 million in 2011 that can pass through again, tax-free! And, any of the maximum exemption from the first person who passed away goes to your beneficiaries... tax-free!

Do you see how transferring jointly held assets to separate trusts can double the money you pass on tax-free?

Be sure to revise your estate plans accordingly keeping in mind that tax laws change.

Now you may be wondering if this set-up avoids lengthy and costly probate. YES, it does if you own the assets in living trusts! This is one of the most ideal ways to set up your assets to save your loved ones and any other heirs the pain, the inconvenience, the frustration, and the taxes and probate expenses they otherwise may have endured!

There are other ways you can own your assets, which we'll review in detail later when we show you how to avoid having your assets taken away due to a lawsuit. But we hope you are at least considering how you own your assets right now!

If you want to KNOW that your surviving spouse and other loved ones are going to be well taken care of when you pass on, then please have a serious talk with your attorney. He or She will work with you to make sure your hard-earned money and assets go to the right people in the most cost efficient way.

Before we wrap up this topic of joint tenancy and how it ties in with estate planning, let's quickly fill you in on one more thing. Let's say you keep your joint tenancy. And, let's say one of you passes away. If the surviving spouse remarries and takes all of these assets, he/she now solely owns and puts them into joint tenancy with the new spouse. And, let's say this surviving spouse now pre-deceases the new spouse. What happens?

This newcomer now owns all of the assets!

And what does that mean to the original family and heirs? Well, depending on the newcomer, they may pass some of it along to them. Or, keep it all. Who knows? The point is, do you really want to hand all of the control of all your assets over to someone "outside" the family?

Probably not, right?

If you want to be in control of your assets and decide who gets what when either of you pass away, then let's start some estate planning immediately. Not for our sake, but for yours and your family!

Otherwise, if you forget, make excuses, or just leave things the way they are without knowing exactly why you set them up that way... you're setting your family and loved ones up for a huge blow!

What type of estate planning should I use?

Since a lot of people perceive estate planning differently, we're going to take you through three critical elements of estate planning, so you can determine what's best for you!

Like all planning, you have to start somewhere.

1) **We recommend that you first start by sitting down with a financial professional to review all of your current assets, your goals, your financial needs and wants, and the hopes and concerns you may have for the future.**

Have this person take a look at where you are today, financially speaking. It's like taking a snapshot and then blowing it up to take a good look at the entire picture. From this point, you can determine exactly where you are today. And this advisor can tell you what will happen to you and your assets if you do nothing.

Now, prepare yourself ahead of time with a list of what you'd like to see happen. Take the advice of what will happen if you do absolutely nothing to your financial portfolio and compare it to this list of desires.

Do they match? Or, are they heading off in totally different directions? If they are not the same, then you need to do some estate planning!

Find yourself a competent retirement advisor who keeps up to speed with all the tax laws, advantages and changes. (From the advice and information you are receiving in this book, we'd suggest that you pull out a few strategies we've shared with you and bring them up with your advisor. If he or she doesn't know what you're talking about, you may want to find-someone else.)

From all the financial advisors and planners we've come in contact with.., let's give you a big tip:

If you start hearing about financial products and canned sales pitches... walk away!

This is not what you need. What you need are alternative suggestions that can lead you to solutions. Your advisor should be able to outline various ways of accomplishing your goals.

Regardless of the techniques, your estate planning attorney and/or advisor will most likely suggest a Will, or a Living Trust, to be the cornerstone of your legal estate planning documents.

And regardless of the size of your estate, you will probably need one of these (a Will or a Living Trust) to memorialize your wishes in writing.

Which one is best?

Well, most attorneys have a preference of one or the other. But for your sake and knowledge, here's what we've found to be the pros and cons of each.

This list is not exclusive, and you shouldn't base your decision on this list alone. We'd strongly recommend that you contact an estate planning attorney to analyze your particular situation. Also, there are several good books just on the pros and cons of Wills and Living Trusts at your local libraries, bookstores and on the Internet.

But for our purposes, let's give you a short-cut education.

WILLS

Pros: Wills are considered simple and easy to create. They are also usually much cheaper than trusts and the other documents that often go with trusts. Now, Wills can be simple or complex based on your personal finances; but, for the most part, they're pretty painless!

Wills don't require the re-titling of your assets in most situations. You'll be asked to assign beneficiaries to your assets, but that's about it.

And most importantly, Wills can be used for certain tax purposes and the naming of guardians for minor children! If you don't select guardians for minor children, and you should by chance pass away while they are still minors, the court will decide where they go...not you!

Cons: The Will you create must go through probate, in most states, if your assets exceed a certain amount. (Probate is the legal term for the process of having the court review your Will and approve its terms.)

Probate fees across the country range from 4-7% of your total assets. Not only do you get zapped with the probate fees, but the real kicker is that it usually takes anywhere from 6-8 months, and often times much longer, depending on your jurisdiction! Each community is different in their probate procedures, but two things remain the same: it's costly, and it takes quite a long time.

Also, another drawback to Wills is that they cannot really address disability issues since Wills don't take effect until you die. This means you may have problems such as who will manage your finances if you become legally disabled or incapacitated. Sometimes a Durable Power of Attorney can solve this. But if not, the whole time you are disabled, your Will cannot go into effect. It only comes into play when you die.

Many people have started to use a "Living Will" that you write before you get sick. And then if you do become disabled, the provisions of the "Living Will" take over, and your wishes are carried out as you instructed. This is for health care issues only, not financial matters.

Just the same, often people think that very simple Wills will cover all of their assets, but joint tenancy rules and beneficiary designations do not follow the distribution rules in the Will! That means those assets will be distributed according to the designation on the specific account...not according to the Will!

(Remember how we pointed out the problem of joint tenancy a few pages back? Remember to analyze your ownership of assets before it may become a problem!)

Let's say you are married and jointly own your home. And let's say your Will has assigned your home to your first son, Tom. Now, your spouse suddenly passes away and the home has now been assigned to you.

You have no way of keeping up with the mortgage payment, utilities and so forth. And on top of it, you become permanently disabled and put into a nursing home or care facility.

What happens to the house? Well, chances are the bank will foreclose on it, and you'll lose it. Or, you'd have to get someone to help sell it for you.

Either way, the house is gone. You either sell and take a loss, or the bank or Medicaid (in some states) gets it. Not your kids, or whoever you left it to in the Will!

When your spouse passed away, because you jointly owned the property, it became yours. And even though you're disabled in a nursing home, the Will cannot go into effect and the property passed on to whomever you want it to go to.

Pretty lousy situation, huh? That's why we list this as a "con," because it is definitely a risk factor in a will!

LIVING TRUSTS

Pros: Living Trusts avoid probate in most states if your assets are fully titled in the Trust.

By avoiding probate fees, you could save thousands of dollars in probate costs, and all the court and attorney fees incurred in the probate process as well as all the time probate takes.

Normally, Living Trusts are much more detailed than a Will in the way your assets will be managed and distributed. They are much more specific and provide a very good framework of leaving instructions to your heirs.

Living Trusts may also avoid problems if you become disabled and if your assets are setup properly in the Trust. This is because a Living Trust can protect your assets if you become disabled.

Living Trusts have become very popular. In many areas, Living Trusts are the preferred estate planning method.

Talk to your estate planning attorney and financial professional about them. Chances are, they will agree that Living Trusts offer more benefits and more specific directions for the disbursement of your assets.

Con: Living Trusts usually cost a bit more than a Will to draw up, but that is because they are much more detailed and involve a lot more work in preparing them.

Although a Living Trust can save you a bundle in probate fees, we wanted to make you aware that only an attorney should prepare it. Several scam artists have gone around the country "selling" Living Trusts. If you bought one of these, chances are you may not be protected. Have a qualified estate planning attorney review your plan.

Also, Living Trusts will ONLY avoid probate or a guardianship if the assets are actually titled into the Trust.

If you leave any assets untitled outside of your Living Trust, they may then still have to go through probate. You really want to keep in mind that if you want full protection of the disbursement of your assets, then title all your assets into the Trust.

This may cause a bit more work on your end, and a bit of preparation time, but it all depends on what you want. It will involve re-titling of all your assets into the Trust, and changing beneficiary designations.

A Will is simple, cheap, and allows you to assign beneficiaries. A Living Trust handles all of your assets, gives you maximum security and eliminates costly probate of your assets.

OTHER ESTATE PLANNING STRATEGIES

While we won't provide complex technical details of advanced estate planning strategies, we would like to briefly discuss some examples of planning techniques that may be of interest:

- **Charitable Remainder Trusts (CRT). We discussed CRTs in Chapter 5 and all the income tax benefits they provide. But that wasn't the whole story! Besides being able to sell assets without paying any capital gains tax, you get two huge estate planning benefits:**

i. You can get a lifetime income from the earnings made off of the assets for the rest of your and your family's life!

91

ii. When you pass away, all of the assets in the Trust are excluded from your estate!

So that, not only do CRTs provide zero capital gains tax when selling assets, they also provide zero estate taxes on those assets!

Here's another amazing part of a CRT. Since the assets inside the Trust are ultimately going to a charity, the kids or grandchildren will not get that portion of the estate. But, since there is usually an income tax savings from the charitable deductions, you can use a small portion of the tax savings to buy a second-to-die life insurance policy with a face amount that's the same amount as the assets put into the CRT! And this life insurance policy can also be estate tax free by putting the policy into an insurance trust!

Now, the younger generations will get the full value of these assets completely estate and income tax free!

A CRT is an amazing tool that most people simply don't know about.

There are various rules you need to be aware of, and planning techniques that one can use in order to accomplish your estate planning goals. Just so you understand, this book is not designed to explain each and every planning technique in detail and how they work. There are many other books that focus just on those issues.

What we want to accomplish is to make you aware that most EVERYONE needs some type of estate planning!

And when you take steps into estate planning, your attorneys and financial advisors can help recommend the various techniques and details that may be available to get you, but it's YOUR job to determine where you want to be!

To help you out, we've prepared a list to assist you ahead of time in answering questions you'll be asked.

Don't worry if you don't have immediate answers. Part of the estate planning process is helping you to answer these questions.

We're just giving you a sneak preview of the many questions so you can start thinking about them TODAY, and then sort through the fine details when you begin the process of estate planning with the professionals you've chosen.

1)   Who do you want to raise your minor children (if applicable) when you pass away? Remember that you should have 2-3 back ups."

2) Who do you want to manage your assets if you become sick or pass away? Again, remember to have "back ups."

3) Who will make any medical decisions for you if you are unable?

4) Who will receive your assets?

5) How will your heirs receive these assets? Will it be in one lump sum or spread out over several years? Or, will they only get the income, with the remainder going to someone else?

6) Who will receive your assets if your primary heirs predecease you? And, how do you want those assets distributed?

7) Do you have any charitable goals in mind?

8) Do you have personal assets (jewelry, mementos, figurines, etc.) that you want a particular person(s) to receive?

9) How important is estate planning to you?

10) Are you willing to give up some control to save thousands in taxes and future legal fees?

11) What is the relationship you have with your children?

12) What assets do you own? What are their fair market values? Do you own them jointly, and if so, with whom? What did you pay for these assets? (Don't forget to Include the value of any life insurance and retirement plans!)

13) How old will your heirs be before they can have access to the money?

Besides the above, there are many more questions that will need to be answered. However, this list should show you the most common questions you'll need to address first.

Your advisor's job is to guide you through the estate planning process from A-Z. And it's also his or her job to ask probing question about your goals and objectives.

YOUR job is to make sure that you have CLEARLY defined goals and objectives!

You should be given plenty of alternatives and full explanations of their benefits or downfalls. It is only from understanding these various techniques that you'll be able to make the best decisions. You'll be able to weigh your options and pave the road to your desired goals.

And oftentimes you'll find that advisors will recommend a combination of techniques in order to achieve your final desired results, which is a good thing.

Just as a doctor may prescribe several medications for different health problems, your advisors will prescribe different planning techniques that work together as part of an overall master plan.

What Will Happen If You Don't Do Proper Estate Planning?

Actually, we have two answers to this question. (We hope you realize by now what a mistake it is not to do proper estate planning!)

1) TAXES: We've already gone over the details, but we just want to repeat how costly and needless these estate taxes are.

2) FEES: Look out...if you do not implement proper estate planning, you'll be shocked at all the fees you and/or your heirs will certainly encounter!

For instance, you could incur unnecessary probate fees, legal fees, guardianship fees, and court costs...just to name a few!

These fees are mostly going to attorneys, but some also go to the court and government.

The sad part is that these fees can mount up to a large percentage of your estate and are mostly a total waste of money!

This is no joke. We've seen many people pay through the nose in unnecessary fees. And the most shocking thing to us is that many of these people weren't even aware of them.

But now you are.

And you have to do something to avoid this from happening. Not tomorrow. Not next week or next year. You must do something right now. And although hiring advisors is not free, it will cost you a heck of a lot more if you don't! In the real world, it will cost you substantially less to protect your assets than if you don't protect them. That's it. End of story.

We hope you see the big picture and do something!

DO-IT-YOURSELF ESTATE PLANNING

Unfortunately, too many people are buying computer programs, books or surfing the Internet for ideas on how to "create their own estate plans." This is as bad as buying a computer program or book on "how to perform your own open-heart surgery!"

94

We're serious. This has become an epidemic that's sure to kill many people's financial picture! And needless to say, it's a very dangerous gamble to take.

Although it may seem less expensive than seeking the advice of competent attorneys, accountants, and other advisors, you'll be dealt a bad hand if you choose to do it yourself.

And even worse than that, many of these programs and their documents may not even be legal in your state!

For example, in these do-it-yourself Living Trust kits that are popping up, in almost every situation, the forms will not meet your requirements. And if they don't meet your requirements, they won't be implemented properly.

Just like you wouldn't get a do-it-yourself kit to perform open-heart surgery on yourself, you shouldn't think that you don't need estate planning attorneys and advisors to help you. Remember it's cheaper to hire a Ph.D. than it is to become one!

This is true not only for you, but for your spouse and your family who will have to hire advisors to fix the problems created by any "home remedy" do-it-yourself estate plan.

All in all, estate planning can seem very complex. The principle of it, however, is not.

As we've taken you through this chapter, we certainly hope that it has hit home with you on how important estate planning is for EVERYONE. The principle is simple...either you plan, manage and control the distribution of your assets for when you pass away... or you don't.

Think about it...

- **You can legally keep the IRS and attorneys out of your pocket and control exactly who gets what from you.**

- **If you own anything, it's an asset.**

- **Estate planning is the building up (accumulation) (ownership), taking care of (management) (set up), and distribution (disbursement) of your assets after you're gone.**

- **What type of estate planning should you use? Sit down with your financial advisor to review all your current assets, goals, financial needs and wants, plus your hopes and concerns for the future.**

- **Be sure your advisor(s) keep up with all the tax laws, advantages and changes.**

- Seek alternative solutions!

- Wills are considered simple and easy to create but must go through probate in most states if your assets exceed a certain amount.

- A Living Trust is more detailed and specific than a Will but avoids probate in most states.

- If you do not plan your estate properly, your estate can be wiped out by:

    1) Taxes - estate taxes and,
    2) Fees - probate, legal, guardianship and court fees!

Chapter 12

INVESTMENTS MADE EASY
(HOW TO MAKE THE RIGHT CHOICES
WITHOUT ANY HYPE)

໖

We've come to a point in this book where we're going to talk about an area of finance that is probably only second in confusion to insurance.

What is it, you ask? Investments.

We can't tell you how many times we see things people have done with investments that just don't make any sense. We see so many people who really don't understand what investing is all about. What investments really are. What they should be, what they shouldn't be. What they can do for you, and what they can't do for you.

Let's talk about investments and give a couple of case studies to illustrate our points.

The first thing we want to do is identify what the word investment really means. If you look in the dictionary, "investment" is defined as "to commit or use money or capital for the purchase of property or a business, etc. with the expectation of profit." Pretty straightforward, right? To expect a profit.

The whole concept behind the term "investment" is for you to take the money you've already made, one way or another, and make it work for you, so it returns more than you started with. It's a pretty simple concept, yet the simplest things are often the most complicated.

Take the case of Wally and Joann. Wally and Joann are married and in their 60's. Wally used to be an accountant for a major manufacturer where he worked for 37 years. Joann didn't work outside the home until their children were grown, and then she took a job as a counselor for a local social work organization.

When they retired a few years ago, they decided they should figure out what to do with the money they had from their IRAs, savings from over the years, money from the sale of their home (they bought a much smaller home after the kids were gone and basically left the money sitting in the bank for quite some time), and other various assets they owned.

When they finally decided to do something about their financial situation, and take care of their investments, they went to see an investment counselor at a large national firm. He told them that for people in their age bracket, they would be best off owning a U.S. government bond fund.

They got a nice brochure and prospectus from the salesperson, with a picture of the American flag and fireworks on the cover, which talked about the fact that 100% of the money invested in this fund would go into U.S. government securities, which were backed by the full faith and credit of the U.S. government. The time was late 1986.

Wally and Joann liked the idea of putting their money in the U.S. government. After all, they felt patriotic and thought the idea of having the full faith and credit of the U.S. government backing their investment was about as safe as you could get. Sounds good, right?

But, while it was never said, and maybe never even implied, there lurked some feeling that these might be "kind of" like CDs -- "kind of" guaranteed because it was an investment dealing with U.S. government obligations.

Anyway, in the spring of 1987, Wally and Joann (along with millions of other Americans) had a major shock. For some reason, interest rates jumped almost two percentage points in a matter of a couple of weeks. Interest rates on things like long-term government bonds, mortgages, etc., moved up with no warning.

Wally and Joann followed the price of their bond fund in the local paper because it was listed with the other investments. One day while Wally was drinking his morning coffee, he called over to Joann in horror to show her the price of their bond fund. It had dropped several dollars a share. In fact, since Wally was an accountant, he quickly figured out it had dropped 19% in value. They were both stunned and thought it must be a mistake.

They immediately called their investment salesman to ask him if there was some problem with the price quoted in the paper. He regretted to inform them that no, there was no mistake. The fund had dropped that much in value but would probably come back.

What they didn't understand was this bond fund was investing in 30-year government bonds and was using a technique to enhance the income the fund was generating, which at the time was touted to be between 10-11%. The combination of the 30-year bonds and the technique the fund used to enhance the income with the sudden rise in interest rates caused the value of the shares to plummet.

Their $100,090 investment was worth barely over $80,000, and they'd only been in the investment for a few months.

98

Yes, they had made a few thousand dollars of interest income over that time, but they had taken that money out and used it to live on. They were devastated. How could this happen? What went wrong?

When they came to get help, the first thing that had to be done (as usual) was look at their whole financial picture. In the course of designing their retirement plan, they needed help dealing with what had happened to the bond fund. The news wasn't so good.

Wally and Joann had encountered a very interesting phenomenon in the world of investments. The law of gravity works on investments just like on objects. Or, in other words, it takes more "energy" to get an investment up, after it's gone down!

When an investment declines in value, it has to increase more than it lost in value as a percentage...just to break-even!

For example, when the stock market caved in 2000, 2001 and 2008...many people lost 50% or more of their stock values. As an illustration, let's say someone you know had put in $100,000 into the market in 2006, and two years later in 2008, the stocks were worth only $50,000. That's a 50% drop in value, right?

Now, if the stocks went back up 50% from the $50,000 value, would that make them whole at a value of $100,000? NO! IT WOULD NOT! A 50% increase in value from $50,000 would only be $25,000...making the stocks worth only $75,000. Still a big loss from the original $100,000.

In order for the $50,000 value of stocks to go back up to $100,000...the stocks would have to increase by 100%. That's right. A 50% loss in stocks would require a 100% gain to get back to even!

Now in Wally and Joann's example of them putting $100,000 in the bond fund, and it dropping 20% down to $80,000. If that $80,000 increased 20%, it would go up $16,000 and they would only have $96,000. It would have to increase 25% to actually get back to the $100,000. As a percentage, it has to go up more than the 20% loss!

This is one of the rules of investing that most people don't think about. Investment salespeople don't like to talk about it because it is so hard for people to make up lost ground on investments that go sour.

Which is why it's so important to do some of the things we're going to discuss later in this chapter, particularly diversification.

The advice given to Wally and Joann was to sit tight because they didn't have an immediate need for the money, and we thought, considering their other assets, it might not be a bad idea to wait and see if things came back.

Fortunately, over a period of years, the funds did eventually come back to the $100,000 they started with. At which time they decided to sell the fund and put the money elsewhere.

They were lucky because they hadn't put all their eggs in one basket.

They're also lucky because the fund did come back.

The real lesson here is that they made an investment decision without first having it done in the context of a plan. And,

They made investment decisions based on fancy brochures and beautiful pictures, with no clue what they were buying or how it worked.

While we're not insinuating that the salesperson misled them in any way, we are saying that the marketing materials and the way the fund was presented to the public certainly gave the impression they were dealing with U.S. Government guaranteed money, when in fact they were not. They were actually dealing with securities, which like all securities, will go up and down in price, sometimes for no apparent reason.

Let's talk about another couple, Barb and Dave. Barb and Dave were both 61 years old. They owned and worked together for years in a retail company that they eventually sold to their manager, Cindy, and retired with a nice chunk of change in their pockets. When Barb and Dave sold the business, like Wally and Joann, they went to see an investment counselor at a large national firm.

In their case, the investment counselor recommended they put the money from the sale of the company into some real estate investments (limited partnerships) that were supposed to have duration of 3-4 years, which was the timeframe they wanted the money available for the particular things they wanted to do (trips, summer home, golf club membership, that sort of thing).

They put the money into the partnerships and several problems occurred. One was because of the general decline of the real estate market, the value of their investments dropped significantly. The second one was, they discovered, there was little or no market for their shares of the investment when they wanted to sell later on, and they were stuck with the investments.

The third problem was they had put almost all of their money into the investments and violated one of the cardinal rules of investing, which, as we will discuss in a minute, is never put all your eggs in one basket.

100

For Barb and Dave, things worked out poorly because they had so much tied up in these investments and couldn't get their money out. And because what they could get out was worth so much less than what they put in, they literally had to change their whole life, change all their plans and had to return to work. In fact, they spent several years working for Cindy in their own store trying to make enough money to keep themselves going.

Now, let's talk about a case study where someone did very well.

Frank and Marci came into get planning assistance for retiring and had no real plan for their retirement.

They had some money they didn't know what to do with and all kinds of questions. We won't go into details about the other areas, but we will discuss what happened with their investment part of the plan.

It was recommended they invest in a diversified group of investments in different areas of the economy. They were given quite a few choices to look at and consider based on the goals and objectives they set forth. Based on the plan and what they were trying to accomplish, they made some decisions and agreed that they should diversify their investment portfolio into various sectors of the economy.

They ended up with a portfolio of different investments. They started off with slightly over $100,000, but for purposes of illustration, let's assume it was exactly $100,000.

Another couple that came in at the same time was Arnold and Vicki. Arnold and Vicki had a similar amount of money as Frank and Marci. They came in to get help with some planning decisions but were not comfortable making any decisions.

Based on the fact that they were unable to make any decisions, except to leave their money in the bank, that's what they did. Again, for purposes of illustration, let's assume they had exactly $100,000 in order to make the math easy.

Frank and Marci chose five different groups or categories of investments, and within each group chose individual investments in that category.

We'll discuss the five categories and show you basically what happened. They chose:

1. Cash
2. Insurance Products
3. Mutual Funds
4. Real Estate
5. Managed Accounts

They put $20,000 into each category to start their investment fund.

Let's look at the following table that will show you what happened over twenty years to those five groups of investments. (Ignoring taxes and commissions for illustration's sake.)

Investment	Starting Value	Gain or Loss	Ending Value (20 years)
1. Cash	$ 20,000	5%	$ 53,066
2. Insurance Products	20,000	7%	77,394
3. Mutual Funds	20,000	13%	230,462
4. Real Estate	20,000	0%	20,000
5. Managed Accounts	20,000	-5%	7,169
Totals	$100,000		$338,091

Isn't that interesting? Some of the investments returned CD-like rates and didn't make much money. Some lost money or only broke-even. Some did pretty well. At the end of 20 years, the total value of their $100,000 was $388,901. If you took that and figured the annual average rate of return, the result is a 7.02% annual compounded rate of return.

Let's talk about Arnold and Vicki.

They took the path of least resistance and put their money in CDs.

At the end of the same 20-year period, their $100,000 was worth $265,330, which translates out to a 5% annual rate of return... and $122,761 less than Frank and Marci.

What happened? Why is their account worth so much less than Frank and Marci's?

What happened was they didn't diversify. They put all their eggs in the CD basket, and there was no chance for the money to do anything more than what CDs are going to do. (Not to mention that the rate of return they made is only being counted before taxes and inflation! If you subtract their tax rate of 25%, and the inflation rate over this period of 5%, they actually have a NEGATIVE rate of return in terms of purchasing power! (We'll be talking more about this in a minute.)

Frank and Marci, on the other hand, diversified their portfolio into five separate groups and then within those five groups had as many as four or five different investments for a few thousand dollars each - a very well-balanced and well-diversified portfolio.

No one can predict the future. If we told you we knew what would happen in the investment world today, tomorrow, next week, next year, we would be lying, and so is anyone else who says they do. There are no crystal balls. No one can tell you what will happen. We would only be guessing, and guessing isn't good enough.

On the other hand, you can't be like Arnold and Vicki and leave your money sitting in the bank, because we know that decision can be costly.

The best solution is to diversify your portfolio based on what your plan calls for, understand the options within each group, make educated choices, keep an eye on things so you know where you stand, and make changes to your investment portfolio and plan as time goes by.

Once you do your planning, many options will become apparent that fit your situation. Other options you may have read about, heard about, or been told about by your brother-in-law, may not fit your situation, because you will see they don't fit into your plan.

Again, planning is crucial.

We think, it's very important for us to point out some very critical areas of investment planning that need to be understood without going into how the specific investments work with technical details and financial mumbo-jumbo.

If you are interested in learning the intricate details of how mutual funds work, or the ins and outs of insurance products and annuities, etc., there are dozens of books you can get at the library or bookstore or websites that will explain everything.

Again, the purpose of this book is not to be a technical manual, but rather to be a useful manual so you can understand your choices and what you can do.

We'll be talking about investment options from a planning perspective, and we think you will see this will help you a great deal in making your final decisions, once you do your planning.

The first area we will cover is the one we referred to as diversification. In fact, if we had to pick one investment principle over all others (behind planning, of course) it would be diversification.

Diversification is simply defined as "spreading your risk out and putting your money in different places" or never "put your eggs in one basket," as the saying goes.

The ancient Greeks understood diversification. When they shipped their goods and grains to other places, they never put all of one grain on one ship. In other words, they didn't put all the barley on one ship, and all the spices on another ship because they understood that if one of those ships sunk, they would lose the entire supply of that item. They understood the benefits of spreading the risk by putting some amount of each item onto each ship. That way, if a ship sunk, they would only lose a part of that item, not the entire amount.

There's nothing new under the sun. Yet, we see so many people who "put all their eggs in one basket," or, in modern terms, all their money in the bank, all their money in mutual funds, all their money in their company stock, etc. (Remember Enron?)

Diversification is absolutely the most fundamental principle of successful investing.

See, there are several aspects of risks in investing we will cover, such as the saying "The higher the risk, the higher the potential return."

Diversification is different. A lack of diversification puts you at more risk yet doesn't necessarily offer you a higher chance of return.

If you remember, Arnold and Vicki did not diversify, and put all their eggs in one basket (the bank), took a much greater risk, and did not get a greater return in exchange for this higher risk.

And, no, putting your money in eight different banks is not considered diversification. Nor is putting all your money in one family of mutual funds, considered diversification.

Diversification means your money is separated by type of investment, by category, by area of the economy or world, geographically or socially. Diversification can be based on maturities, income streams, any number of factors.

Whatever you choose to do, please do not violate this rule by not diversifying. You must be diversified. Diversification equals safety. It protects you against unknown and unforeseen changes in the economy and the financial world. If things go bad in one area it is likely they will go up in another area. If the stock market is down, gold prices might be up. If CDs are paying more, bonds might be down.

There's always give and take in the world of investments just like everything in life.

We cannot stress enough how crucial diversification and spreading out your risk is. If you don't get anything else from this chapter, we hope this point sinks in. In today's lightning fast world of change, spreading out your investments isn't optional. It MUST be the cornerstone of your investment planning!

The next area we have to be concerned with is the idea of risk.

Risk is a misunderstood concept, which most people think of in the wrong way.

People think of risk as putting money in an investment and having their principal value reduced or lost. (Like Wally and Joann experienced when they put their money into the bond fund that lost $20,000 in a few months.)

All this is true of one type of risk, but we need to briefly explain how we think risk really works and how you should think of it.

There are several types of risk in the investment world that we're going to discuss. Now, keep in mind that we're not trying to create a doctoral thesis on the explanation of risk. There are hundreds of theories and hypotheses on how many kinds of risk there are, what they are, how they can be measured and quantified, etc.

But, we're here to talk about YOUR world and life, not some professor's viewpoint on the measurement of risk calculations.

And accordingly, the discussion of risk is meant to be brief, realistic and USEFUL to you.

The first type of risk we just mentioned is the risk of loss of principal. This is a pretty easy risk to understand. This is the type of risk where, for example, you put money into an investment at $10 a share and it goes down to $2 a share and you've lost $8 a share on your principal because of the change in value. These changes in value can occur for all kinds of reasons, such as, market changes, interest rate changes, economic changes, government changes in tax laws or other laws, etc.-- there are all kinds of reasons for you to lose your principal.

Another kind of risk is the risk of loss of purchasing power. Or, another way of saying it is the risk that inflation will destroy the value of your money. If you buy stock at $10 and it goes down to $2, it is a loss of principal if you sell. A real loss of money. That is an easy one for people to see and understand. Even though they don't like it, it is comprehensible and makes sense. But, the loss of purchasing power, just as surely destroys your principal and causes you to lose money, however, is not understood by most people because it is not as easily seen!

In the earlier Chapter 4, we talked about Grandma Hannah whose pension and Social Security income became less and less valuable, which is the same as losing principal in a stock that went down. There's no difference.

If inflation causes things to be more expensive, the money you have is worth less, and it is a financial loss just like a loss from any other risk!

The risk of losing money due to inflation is the most misunderstood and largest risk retirees face.

And, in our opinion, it destroys Americans' retirement security more often than the loss of principal!

Most people do a good job of investing to protect at least some of their assets from the loss of principal; however, very few people understand the risk of loss of purchasing power.

We've covered the details of inflation, so we won't repeat all that here. But, we do want to stress that inflation's destructive power over your financial life and security is probably the most underestimated risk you face.

Another risk people don't understand is the risk of taxation. Yes, that's right. Anything that causes you to lose money is a risk. If you lose money to income taxes, estate taxes or gift taxes, etc., you have again lost money and principal. If you sell an investment for $10,000 and paid $2,500 in taxes, and you keep only $7,500 -- haven't you lost 25% of your asset?

Isn't losing 25% of your asset a loss of principal? It is no different a risk than any other, but also a very misunderstood risk.

It's why tax planning is so critical and important. That's why you must use planning to figure out what your situation is and find out what tax strategies are available to you so you can reduce your taxes as low as possible.

The way you invest your money will have an enormous impact on this risk of losing money from taxation.

Keep in mind that this risk of losing money to taxes is very much under your own control!

Unlike the risk of losing value because the principal (price) drops on a security, which is out of your control, the amount you pay in taxes IS under your control.

For example, you could invest in a CD and choose to pay the maximum amount of tax possible. Or, you could choose to have money in an IRA or annuity and have the taxes on the income deferred until some point in the future. (Deferring taxes doesn't eliminate them, but the compounding effect of having an investment's tax deferred earnings re-invested, as opposed to having taxes paid along the way, will build a much larger value over time!)

Some investments are tax-free. Things like municipal bonds, for example.

Now, we're not saying one of these types of investment is better than another. We are not advocating you run out and switch your investments and savings after reading this.

**What we are saying is that you have to
understand that the risk of taxation is real,
that YOU choose how much of this risk you face,
and how much you'll expect to live with.**

Buy low, sell high -- ingrain that into your brain.

You don't want to "wait" to see what an investment is going to do before you decide to buy in. Particularly if you're waiting for it to go up. If you are going to wait, you should wait until it goes down and then make your purchase.

This leads us to another point about investments that's very important. If you're going to buy any type of security, whether mutual funds of any type, stocks, bonds, etc., the concept of dollar cost averaging is very important. Dollar cost averaging is a way for you to buy investments at a regular interval, on a regular basis, putting in the same amount of money each time, and buying shares at all different prices. What normally happens is that, over time, you'll average out higher and lower prices and have a generally lower cost per share than if you bought the security all at once.

So, for example, if you have $1,200 that your plan says should be in mutual funds, you have two ways to invest.

One way would be to invest the whole $1,200 at one time, at whatever the price is at that point in time, and take your chances that it was the right time to buy. If the fund drops in value after you buy, you'll be aggravated that you didn't wait. If it goes up in value after you buy, you'll be pleased.

But, this approach is more like flipping coins to choose your investment strategy. Heads you win, tails you lose. There's a different and (we think) much better way, Dollar Cost Averaging.

Instead of putting that hypothetical $1,200 in the mutual fund all at once, you could put $100 each month into the fund, for twelve months.

That way, if the shares dropped in price after the beginning of the investment period, you'd be buying MORE shares with each deposit. Also, if the price drop occurred after the first deposit, for example, you would have only put in a small amount ($100) that was subject to the loss...instead of $1,200! Make sense? (The following table illustrates the point.)

(Note: Dollar Cost Averaging Plans involve continuous investment in securities - regardless of fluctuating price levels of such securities. The investor should consider his/her financial ability to continue to purchase through periods of low price levels. Dollar Cost Averaging does not guarantee a profit.)

When you put in $100 per month and you maintain that pattern, you will be buying shares at all different prices - up, down, your contribution remains the same. When prices are up, your money will buy fewer shares, and when share prices are down, your money will buy more shares.

In the following table, the investor had the choice of putting $1,200 at one time, or splitting up the investment using dollar cost averaging. If he had put all the cash in at once, he would have bought 100 shares at $12.

If he spread out the risk using averaging, and the share prices fluctuated, as shown on the table, he would have still invested the same $1,200 but would have bought more shares in the months that prices dropped, and less shares the months the prices went up.

In this example, the investor ends up with 223 shares, at an average price of $5.38 per share (Fund B), instead of 82 shares with an average price of $14.63 per share (Fund A)!

What this process does is provide you with an overall lower cost per share than if you took the money all at one time and placed it into that same investment. It also protects you against ups and downs of prices, so if the stock or fund drops in price, you may actually be happy because you'll be buying more shares.

If you think it will eventually come back up, you'll have all those extra shares at the higher price. Usually this is a much better way to invest in any kind of security than just depositing a lump sum, especially if the market is high. If the market is at all-time lows, it may be more sensible to take lump sums of money and put it in. If the market is moving down or has been-up for a while, dollar cost averaging may make a lot of sense.

THE MAGIC OF DOLLAR-COST-AVERAGING

WHICH ONE WOULD YOU PREFER?

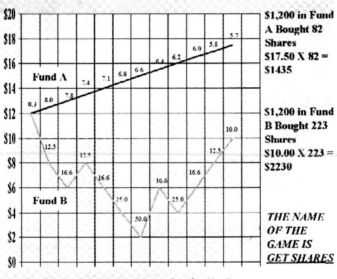

$1,200 in Fund A Bought 82 Shares

$17.50 X 82 = $1435

$1,200 in Fund B Bought 223 Shares

$10.00 X 223 = $2230

THE NAME OF THE GAME IS GET SHARES

Jan Feb Mar Apr May Jun Jul Aug Sept Oct Nov Dec

The advantage of dollar-cost-averaging only accrue if you have the financial ability to continue monthly payments regardless of price levels for an investment that fluctuates in value. Naturally, if you discontinue your payments when the market value of your accumulated shares is less than cost, you will incur a loss. While no investment programs can assure against a loss in declining markets, this systematic method provides a way of investing that has proved it's value when faithfully followed in both good times and bad. Dollar cost averaging also works in reverse when you sell securities. In the case of Art and Betty, who had a lump sum of securities they needed to diversify, it may not have made sense to sell it all at one time but rather to sell the same amount of dollars over an equal period of time, such as each month or each quarter, so they would be selling at various price levels and taking advantage of the ups and downs of the market.

If they had been doing dollar cost averaging on the sales side and that big drop occurred, it would not have hurt them as badly because they would have been selling the shares over a period of time at the higher prices and could have decided whether or not to continue selling when the share prices were lower.

We hope you get the idea from this chapter that investment management and investment options require mostly common sense.

A great measure of common sense and little technical knowledge about investments will serve you much better than extraordinary technical knowledge about investments and little common sense.

Some people in the investment world make things very confusing and complicated and the result is the average person doesn't know what's going on.

Our point is that getting the technical knowledge is easy. Coming up with the common sense techniques we just talked about is very difficult and very rare. Now that you've been made aware of those techniques, hopefully you will integrate them into your planning and understand that some of these investment principles we've discussed go back thousands of years...and are nothing new.

You need to also understand that "guarantees" oftentimes may eliminate or reduce one type of risk, but can cause even greater risks. The best example is bank money, such as CDs, savings accounts, etc., where you do have a guarantee of your principal, but you have no guarantees against loss of purchasing power, or loss by taxation.

We are not saying you shouldn't keep money in the bank.

People should have reserves and some money in the bank, but notice we said "some," not "all."

You need to have a diversified portfolio and investments that will provide you the income, opportunity for growth, hedges against inflation, and give you the best chance of realizing your goals so you can have a secure and peaceful retirement! Using this common sense approach to investing should allow you to sleep peacefully at night, which, after all, is the whole point!

Think about it….

- **"Investment" is defined as "to commit or use money or capital for the purchase of property or a business, etc. with the expectation of profit."**

- **"Diversification" is defined as "separating your money by type of investment, category, area of the economy or world, geographically or** socially. Diversification can be based on maturities, income streams, or any number of other factors.

- You must diversify your investments. Diversification is the most fundamental principle of successful investing. A lack of diversification puts you at more risk; yet doesn't offer you a higher chance of return.

- Do not put all your eggs in one basket.

- Risk:

  - Risk of loss of principal.

  - Risk of loss of purchasing power, i.e., inflation.

  - Risk of losing money due to inflation is the most misunderstood and largest risk retirees face. It can destroy their retirement security more often than the loss of principal. And because of the astronomical rate of inflation in the medical field, (14% annually), an extended stay in a Long Term Care facility has become the number 1 threat to wiping out your nest egg according to SmartMoney.com (9/08)

  - Risk of taxation.

Chapter 13

THE TRUTH ABOUT INSURANCE

∞

We're going to start off this chapter on insurance with a little story about just how much of a problem it can be understanding and dealing with insurance.

We are going to give you some simple facts about insurance that you need to know and tell you what kind of insurance you should have and what kind you shouldn't have.

We'll share a couple of case studies with you about people who have had problems with insurance. You can see what they have done wrong and not repeat the same mistakes for yourself.

There aren't too many financial topics that aggravate people more than insurance.

No one can survive in today's world without having different types of insurance. Insurance, in and of itself, isn't so bad. In fact, in many cases it's necessary. But to be candid, the insurance industry has caused itself all kinds of problems because of the way it has made things as confusing as possible, and made it generally unpleasant to deal with insurance companies.

It is a topic that most people have negative feelings about.

So, here we are, faced with a fact of life we have to deal with.

So what can you do? How do you make sure you are covered correctly and not have to put up with a bunch of sales hype and baloney?

Take Fred and Carla's story for example. Fred and Carla were in their mid 60's. Fred was 63 and Carla was 62. He was a retired engineer who quit working a few months ago. Carla was a seamstress and did sewing on the side for people in the neighborhood.

She's never really went out and advertised her services, but being in the neighborhood as long as she was, people knew when they needed pants hemmed or somebody gained weight and needed pants let out, or someone needed a wedding dress adjusted or bridesmaid gowns made up, Carla was the person to go to.

They raised two kids, Bob and Cheryl. Both were living on their own with their families.

Fred and Carla had six grandchildren, their most recent being born a few months ago about the same time Fred retired.

When they came in for planning, they were concerned about the fact that Fred had just recently retired and wanted to know if they were set up properly.

They also wanted answers to questions about their health insurance because Fred, not yet 65, didn't qualify for Medicare and wasn't sure what he should do about health insurance. They didn't know if it would be better to stay with, and pay for, the plan through work, get his own coverage, go with an HMO, PPO, etc.

When they came in for planning, they were truly quite confused. They heard one thing about insurance from their brother-in-law, Tom, who is an insurance agent. They also heard about insurance from people in the personnel office at work. They read about insurance from articles in AARP and Money Magazine. They listened to other seniors and retirees talking about what they'd done with their insurance.

They admitted they had no idea what to do.

As we described earlier, the first thing we had to do was get a handle on where they were today. We had to first get an assessment of what they had before we could even begin to help in any way. We asked them to dig through the drawers, envelopes, make a visit to the safe deposit box, etc., and gather all their policies together to bring in.

On their second visit to the office, they brought in all their insurance policies. Fred had an old whole-life policy that he bought in 1957, when Bob was born. It was a $5,000 face value policy that had a few thousand dollars of cash value still saved up. In fact, Fred was still paying the premiums on the policy that were $374 a year.

He also had a bigger whole-life policy they had bought when Cheryl was born, which had a $12,000 face value. It didn't have much cash value left because they had borrowed most of it out over the years for different purposes, particularly for the kid's education. The annual premium on that policy was $566.

Carla had no insurance on her life. When we asked them why, they said they didn't know exactly, but they had read that only the man should have life insurance since his pension is usually bigger and there's a bigger loss to the wife if the husband dies first. (Boy, wait `til you see how these rules of thumb, read in a magazine, or heard on a radio talk show, are so dangerous!)

They also had a whole-life policy for $23,000 that was supposed to cover their mortgage. This policy was on Fred's life and carried an annual premium of $820. The cash value of $12,300 was still sitting in the policy. They had never touched it, hoping to save it for the future.

113

In addition, they had two basic coverage type auto policies -- one on each car. They also had a typical homeowner's policy from the same agent they had their car insurance with. And, they were currently covered under the group health insurance plan that Bob had at work, which he was able to keep paying for, with a premium of $512 per month.

That was their insurance coverage, as it existed when they came in.

Now we won't bore you and go into all the tiny details of each policy. But, for purposes of illustrating how confusing insurance can be, we want to go through this with you and help you see what they were doing wrong, how they could fix it, and how their insurance problems were the most common problems people have with insurance. (Maybe the same you have with your insurance?)

In order to understand what you should do about life insurance, if you should get some, get rid of what you have, keep what you have, change what you have, and so on. We need to go to the absolute basics.

These are some very basic principles. Principles that Fred and Carla had not followed and needed to be thinking about very carefully.

Before we start our analysis, let's go into a brief discussion about what life insurance is all about.

This will be no great mystery or shock to anybody when we tell you that the purpose of life insurance, and the only purpose, is to provide money for the family, or other interested entity like a business or charity, in the event of someone's death.

Now, within that explanation there are all kinds of people who fall into the category we'll call the "under-insured."

We can have one, or both spouses in the family who are providing income, and if they passed away, that income would be lost. This is what's known as the "replacing the breadwinner" reason for buying life insurance.

There also can be reasons for buying life insurance like Fred and Carla-- to pay off debts, mortgages, business loans, etc.

Sometimes people buy life insurance when they're in business so funds would be available to buy out a partner's family, if one partner passed away. Life insurance can be used to pay estate taxes. Life insurance can be used to leave money behind for family members, for education and so forth.

There are many reasons why people decide to buy life insurance.

**The bottom line is that life insurance is there
to provide money when someone passes away.**

That's it!

The industry has developed many types of policies over the years. But, when you get right down to the bottom line, there are only two main categories of policies:

1) Cash value policies. Policies that have a savings account of some kind in addition to the insurance protection.

2) Term policies. No cash values, just pure insurance like most other kinds. If you don't use it, you lose it!

In the first category, there are Whole Life policies or other forms of cash value policies like Universal Life policies, Variable Life policies, Increasing Premium Whole Life policies, Paid-Up policies, Deposit Term policies, Vanishing Premium policies, Single Premium policies, etc., etc., etc. Dozens of types of policies.

In the second category, there are literally dozens of types of term insurance as well. It's called "term" because, usually, the policy stays in force for a fixed period of time, without any savings component. They can be Increasing Premium Annual Term, Ten Year Term, Twenty Year Term, (or any other number of years), Decreasing Term, Modified Whole Life Term, etc. The list is almost endless.

The point is, while there are many individually packaged products, there are only two basic kinds of life insurance.

Cash value or no cash value.

That's it.

They can call it different things. But, life insurance is still life insurance, no matter what it's called. They are all just variations of the two kinds that exist.

That's it.

Now given all that information, Fred and Carla had to analyze one question and one question only:

**If either of them were to die, is there a need for more money
than the family currently has available to it
from savings and investments?**

That's the only question. That's the only question you have to ask. That's it.

Ask yourself, "If you and/or your spouse were to pass away, is there a need for more money than you currently have available through your savings and investments?"

We'll come back to our discussion of the types of policies in more detail in a minute. Right now, we want to review how much life insurance someone needs, if any.

For example, let us tell you a story about a couple who didn't need any life insurance.

Let's look at Martin and Terry. They were in their late 60's, had recently sold a business, and after paying their taxes had over $1 million in cash, stocks, IRAs, pensions, etc. and were truly financially independent.

When we talked to them about estate planning and their life insurance situation, they told us they weren't concerned about their three children who all had college educations and made very good money. All three of the children's spouses also worked and were set financially. The grandchildren's college educations were being planned for, and paid for, by their children.

Martin and Terry had no mortgage on their house, no mortgage on their vacation home, no mortgage or debts on their boat. In other words, they were set. Their monthly income from their pensions and Social Security was $3,556 per month and their real monthly expenses (which they had to pay, i.e. property taxes, etc.) only ran $800-1,000 per month.

They had a significant excess cash flow each month, not to mention all the money in the bank and other investments. The $3,556 fixed income they were receiving did not even include what they received from their investments.

They were willing to sign a waiver with us stating that they were not concerned about their estate taxes, that they weren't willing to give up any control of their current assets seeing that they were still young and healthy, felt their children were set, did not feel they owed their children any money, and really had no reason to feel anyone would be "left behind" when they passed away.

Since they didn't care about estate taxes either, this was a perfect example of a couple that really did not need any life insurance.

If either of them were to pass away, the heirs would have plenty of money from their estate to take care of the taxes and have money left over.

Other people may disagree and say they should buy insurance to protect the estate from taxes so their kids would get more, but in their case, they didn't want to do it. It's their choice not to care about estate taxes. Not ours.

When Martin and Terry came in, they were spending $2,782 a year on some life insurance policies that we advised them to get rid of because that $2,782 a year was being wasted. They agreed, and subsequently canceled their policies.

Now, that's their situation. It has nothing to do with Fred and Carla's or yours. We are just illustrating their story to point out that not everybody needs life insurance (contrary to what the life insurance industry will tell you).

If someone has enough assets to take care of the survivors without extra money from the insurance, if they don't care about estate taxes, if they don't have a need for business purposes, they don't need life insurance. It's just that simple.

But that's Martin and Terry. They are the exception. Many people do need life insurance because they either need, or want, to have more money available for their survivors when they pass away.

People like Fred and Carla.

In Fred and Carla's case, we first had to analyze what resources they had available, so when one of them passed away, we could project the subsequent effect on their income and assets.

We had to take a look at the fact that when Fred passed away, how much money would Carla get each month from the remainder of his pension that she was entitled to, plus her Social Security income? We also needed to know how much income she would have from their current investments and savings (that total $109,000, give or take a couple of dollars.)

But, before we did that, we had to figure out how much money she would need before seeing if what she already had would be enough.

Now what if, for example, she needed $2,000 a month to live on (if Fred were to pass away) in today's dollars. Is there any need for life insurance on Fred's life? He agreed he'd need approximately the same $2,000 a month to live on if Carla were to pass away as well.

So, let's take the reverse. What if Carla were to pass away? Fred would have slightly more money coming in each month since his pension was higher than hers.

So, for right now, they would both have enough money coming in in the event of either of them dying.

So would you say they don't need any life insurance? (Hint -remember these figures we're giving you are in today's dollars!)

We had to crunch the numbers through our computer program to show them that if they lived to age 90 (which is a realistic way to plan), would either or both of them be OK? When we do life insurance planning, we always assume the people would die tomorrow because we don't know what other assumption is valid. (Now granted, they probably would not have died the next day, but we have to plan that way to be conservative.)

Would their assets and pension be enough? Would they need any life insurance? If so, how much, and should they keep what they have?
Would there be any difference between how much Fred would need versus how much Carla would need?

Would they have enough in the early years, only to be wiped out because inflation would cause them to start dipping into their principal?

These are all good questions.

When we did crunch the numbers, taking into account the income they needed, building inflation into it, the assets they had, the earnings on those assets, Social Security income, pension, their debts, liabilities and so forth, the computer cranked out that Fred needed about $384,000 of coverage if Carla were to die, and that Carla needed about $295,000 of coverage if Fred died before her. (See the tables on the following pages).

So the first step is always to figure out how much insurance you need, at this point ignoring what policies you have already because those are irrelevant until the right AMOUNT of coverage is determined.

The graphs and tables show the picture very clearly. The graph's solid areas show their available capital while the line shows their need. The area beneath the line is their shortfall.

These pictures demonstrate just how critical it is to crunch the numbers with a scientific approach. No hype, just the math.

And, as you can see, their insurance needs decrease as time goes on. However, insurance is the only way to cover that shortfall in the meantime.

This analysis is crucial because you may find out you're over insured, underinsured, or just fine. Whichever way it goes, at least you have the answers based on sound, prudent planning instead of some salesperson making up a "formula" (translation "guess") about how much coverage you need!

That's the important part.

Now we have to look at what policies they already had. Does what the computer tell them they need match up to what they had? In fact, they both had the wrong amounts of insurance, which was very important. The printouts and graphs show they were both underinsured.

Not only that, but the policies they had were old and out-of-date policies, providing meager cash value increases, paying very low interest, with very high premiums (compared to more modern policies).

So, first we established that they needed to change the amount of insurance they had. Secondly, we had to take a look at the kind of insurance they had, what kind of policies they owned, what they were costing, and whether these old policies were the most cost-effective way to handle their needs.

In their case, we recommended they change the policies they had on Fred (since he was in good health) to more cost-effective, newer type policies.

Keep in mind that not everyone has the option of changing to new policies, even if they want to. Their health may not be good enough to warrant a switch. Or, their old policies may be bad, but replacing them wouldn't make financial sense. The only way you can know is to do an analysis based on objective facts, not sales hype!

Survivor Capital Projection for FRED

FRED AND CARLA SAMPLE

	Income needed and sources							Net++	Total
Age	Annual personal expenses*	Earned income (after tax)	Social Security & pensions	Other income or (expense)	Income surplus or (shortage)	Capital needed for income	Immediate cash needs	assets +monthly additions	life insurance needed
43	(32,640)		2,040	(15,000)	(45,600)	(509,789)	(16,593)	92,000	434,381
44	(27,432)		2,040	(15,450)	(40,842)	(496,851)	(16,988)	82,575	430,463
45	(28,250)		2,040	(7,557)	(34,167)	(486,212)	(17,363)	72,761	430,813
46	(29,095)		2,040	(8,195)	(35,251)	(482,433)	(17,730)	70,308	429,876
47	(29,968)		2,040		(27,928)	(477,335)	(18,150)	67,458	428,027
48	(30,870)		2,040		(28,830)	(479,240)	(18,569)	73,267	429,557
49	(29,840)		2,040		(27,800)	(480,362)	(18,991)	79,575	419,775
50	(30,124)		2,040		(28,084)	(482,585)	(19,432)	86,435	415,582
51	(31,118)		2,040		(29,078)	(484,662)	(19,887)	93,887	410,663
52	(32,145)		2,040		(30,105)	(485,876)	(20,358)	101,983	404,250
53	(33,206)		2,040		(31,166)	(486,138)	(20,844)	110,782	396,200
54	(34,302)		2,040		(32,262)	(485,356)	(21,347)	120,344	388,359
55	(35,434)		2,040		(33,394)	(483,429)	(21,865)	130,734	374,560
56	(36,603)		2,040		(34,563)	(480,249)	(22,401)	142,025	360,624
57	(37,811)		2,040		(35,771)	(475,702)	(22,955)	154,298	344,358
58	(39,059)		2,040		(37,019)	(469,663)	(23,527)	167,036	325,553
59	(40,347)		2,040		(38,307)	(461,998)	(24,118)	182,132	303,983
60	(41,679)		2,040		(39,639)	(452,585)	(24,728)	197,888	279,405
61	(43,054)		2,040		(41,014)	(441,212)	(25,358)	215,013	251,557
62	(44,475)		2,040		(42,435)	(427,771)	(26,009)	233,626	220,156
63	(45,943)		2,040		(43,903)	(412,074)	(26,682)	253,859	184,897
64	(47,459)		2,040		(45,419)	(393,826)	(27,377)	275,852	145,451
65	(49,025)		31,091		(17,934)	(373,127)	(28,095)	299,758	101,464
66	(50,643)		31,487		(19,156)	(378,513)	(28,836)	315,452	91,898
67	(52,314)		31,890		(20,424)	(383,814)	(29,602)	331,319	81,298
68	(54,040)		32,301		(21,740)	(386,529)	(30,394)	347,342	69,580
69	(55,824)		32,719		(23,105)	(388,947)	(31,211)	363,505	56,653
70	(57,666)		33,145		(24,521)	(390,151)	(32,055)	379,788	42,419
71	(59,569)		33,579		(25,990)	(390,015)	(32,927)	396,169	26,773
72	(61,535)		34,021		(27,514)	(388,401)	(33,828)	412,485	9,765
73	(63,565)		34,471		(29,094)	(385,162)	(34,759)	428,614	
74	(65,661)		34,930		(30,731)	(380,141)	(35,721)	444,553	
75	(67,830)		35,396		(32,434)	(373,166)	(36,714)	460,191	
76	(70,068)		35,872		(34,196)	(364,055)	(37,740)	475,475	
77	(72,381)		36,350		(36,024)	(352,612)	(38,799)	491,288	
78	(74,769)		36,850		(37,919)	(338,626)	(39,894)	504,525	
79	(77,237)		37,352		(39,884)	(321,871)	(41,025)	518,106	
80	(79,785)		37,864		(41,921)	(302,104)	(42,193)	530,873	
81	(82,418)		38,385		(44,033)	(279,064)	(43,400)	542,703	
82	(85,138)		38,916		(46,222)	(252,472)	(44,647)	553,443	
83	(87,948)		39,457		(48,491)	(222,029)	(45,934)	562,929	
84	(90,850)		40,007		(50,843)	(187,415)	(47,205)	570,981	
85	(93,848)		40,568		(53,280)	(148,286)	(48,639)	577,853	
86	(96,945)		41,139		(55,805)	(104,274)	(50,058)	582,916	
87	(100,144)		41,721		(58,423)	(54,986)	(51,529)	585,939	

* Includes basic personal expenses plus insurance premiums, debt payments and itemized deductions
** Retirement account values (IRA, 401k, etc.) are reduced by 15.00% to account for income taxes

FRED AND CARLA SAMPLE

		Income needed and sources						Net assets ++ +monthly add'ns	Total life insurance needed
Age	Annual personal expenses*	Earned income (after tax)	Social Security & pensions	Other income or (expense)	Income surplus or (shortage)	Capital needed for income	Immediate cash needs		
42	(32,640)		5,100	(15,000)	(42,540)	(466,524)	(20,701)	92,000	395,224
43	(27,432)		5,100	(15,450)	(37,782)	(453,142)	(21,509)	83,576	392,075
44	(28,250)		5,100	(7,957)	(31,107)	(443,681)	(21,584)	72,761	392,504
45	(29,095)		5,100	(8,195)	(32,191)	(440,304)	(21,913)	78,308	391,909
46	(28,968)		5,100		(24,868)	(435,632)	(22,343)	67,458	390,417
47	(30,870)		5,100		(25,770)	(437,991)	(22,870)	73,267	387,595
48	(29,840)		5,100		(24,740)	(439,596)	(23,529)	79,578	383,547
49	(30,124)		5,100		(25,024)	(442,331)	(24,222)	86,435	380,118
50	(31,118)		5,100		(26,018)	(444,952)	(64,952)	92,887	376,818
51	(32,145)		5,100		(27,045)	(446,744)	(25,721)	101,983	370,481
52	(33,206)		5,100		(28,106)	(447,620)	(26,551)	110,782	363,369
53	(34,302)		5,100		(29,202)	(447,490)	(27,326)	120,344	354,533
54	(35,434)		5,100		(30,334)	(446,257)	(28,288)	130,734	343,810
55	(36,603)		5,100		(31,503)	(443,814)	(29,240)	142,026	331,028
56	(37,811)		5,100		(32,711)	(440,050)	(30,246)	154,295	315,997
57	(39,059)		5,100		(33,959)	(434,342)	(31,310)	167,636	298,516
58	(40,347)		5,100		(35,247)	(428,061)	(32,436)	182,132	278,365
59	(41,679)		5,100		(36,579)	(419,568)	(33,628)	197,888	255,308
60	(43,054)		24,988		(18,067)	(409,212)	(34,851)	215,013	229,890
61	(44,475)		25,356		(19,119)	(416,721)	(36,230)	233,626	218,324
62	(45,943)		25,731		(20,212)	(423,647)	(37,690)	253,859	207,138
63	(47,459)		26,112		(21,347)	(429,912)	(39,158)	275,852	193,219
64	(49,025)		30,581		(18,444)	(435,435)	(40,760)	299,758	176,437
65	(50,643)		30,977		(19,666)	(444,205)	(42,116)	315,452	170,570
66	(52,314)		31,380		(20,934)	(452,302)	(43,510)	331,319	164,493
67	(54,046)		31,791		(22,250)	(459,637)	(44,943)	347,342	157,237
68	(55,824)		32,209		(23,615)	(466,114)	(46,416)	363,505	149,026
69	(57,660)		32,635		(25,031)	(471,632)	(47,931)	379,780	139,775
70	(58,569)		33,069		(26,500)	(476,078)	(49,488)	396,169	129,397
71	(61,335)		33,511		(28,024)	(479,333)	(51,000)	412,465	117,868
72	(63,565)		33,961		(29,604)	(481,267)	(52,536)	428,614	105,189
73	(65,663)		34,420		(31,244)	(481,742)	(54,096)	444,550	91,288
74	(67,830)		34,886		(32,944)	(480,607)	(55,678)	460,198	76,087
75	(70,068)		35,362		(34,706)	(477,702)	(57,278)	475,475	59,505
76	(72,381)		35,846		(36,534)	(472,852)	(58,896)	490,288	41,488
77	(74,769)		36,340		(38,429)	(465,871)	(60,527)	504,536	21,862
78	(77,237)		36,842		(40,394)	(456,559)	(62,169)	518,106	622
79	(79,785)		37,354		(42,431)	(444,699)	(63,818)	530,873	
80	(82,418)		37,875		(44,543)	(430,061)	(65,471)	543,703	
81	(85,138)		38,406		(46,732)	(412,397)	(67,121)	555,343	
82	(37,948)		38,947		(49,001)	(391,440)	(68,786)	562,929	
83	(90,850)		39,497		(51,353)	(366,904)	(70,397)	570,980	
84	(93,848)		40,058		(53,790)	(338,483)	(72,025)	577,853	
85	(96,945)		40,629		(56,315)	(305,848)	(73,650)	582,916	
86	(100,144)		41,211		(58,933)	(268,648)	(71,955)	585,936	
87	(103,449)		41,804		(61,645)	(226,506)	(77,765)	718,153	
88	(106,863)		42,407		(64,455)	(179,018)	(79,611)	727,291	
89	(110,389)		43,022		(67,367)	(125,751)	(81,443)	734,826	
90	(114,032)		43,648		(70,384)	(66,244)	(83,254)	740,543	
91									
92									
93									
94									
95									
96									
97									
98									
99									
100									
	J1		J3	J3	J4		J2	O	

* Includes basic personal expenses plus insurance premiums, debt payments and itemized deductions.
** Retirement account values (IRA, 401k, etc.) are reduced by 15.00% to account for income taxes

LIFE INSURANCE

LIFE INSURANCE

FRED AND CARLA SAMPLE

CARLA survives

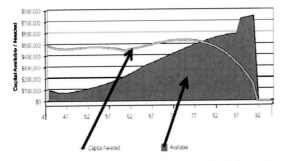

The shaded area of the graph shows the amount of capital available at a given age. The line represents the amount of funds needed to provide capital for immediate cash needs and income for the survivor. If at any time the line extends above the shaded area, this indicates an amount of additional capital needed in the form of insurance.

The graph is interpreted to show the amount of insurance needed if death occurs at a selected age. For example, if no shortage is shown now, then the amount of capital available now will be adequate through life expectancy. If a shortage is indicated 10 years from now, then the additional insurance will be required only if death occurs at that age.

FRED survives

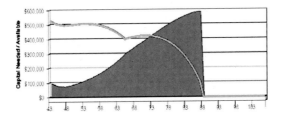

LIFE INSURANCE

In order to assure financial security in the event of the premature loss of a principal wage earner, any surviving heirs must have either an adequate source of wages or they must have sufficient accumulated capital to provide income in the form of interest, dividends, or the ability to consume such capital.

Unless you have already accumulated sufficient capital, the only course of action is to "option" for a sum of money for delivery at the time it is most needed -- the passing of a principal wage earner. The concept of optioning capital is nothing more than the idea of life insurance.

Total amount of capital needed for cash and income.	**Balance needed in the form of insurance**	Life insurance needed is equal to the difference between the capital required for immediate cash needs plus income requirements . . .
	Capital available	. . . LESS the capital available from savings and investments, or the capital equivalent of Social Security and other income sources.

CAPITAL NEEDED (for survivor income and expenses)
As time passes and the remaining heirs become less dependent on the wage earner, the total capital needed usually decreases.

CAPITAL AVAILABLE (savings and investments)
If a careful program of saving and investing is followed, then capital available grows. At the point where the CAPITAL AVAILABLE is equal to the CAPITAL NEEDED, then life insurance is no longer needed except in cases where assets are not liquid.

In preparing the following Survivor Capital reports, all income needed and available has been converted to an equivalent "Present Value Capital" amount. In other words, we show the amount of capital that would be needed today to provide the future stream of income assuming that the capital will earn interest at 6.25% and be fully consumed at the end of the period shown or at life expectancy.

Note: Projected insurance requirements can vary over time due to changes in asset levels, special expenses, education expenses, estate planning and spouse retirement needs. Additional insurance, held outside of an insurance trust, may have estate tax consequences. It may be prudent to purchase an amount of insurance appropriate to prepare for projected higher coverage needs. Consult with your financial and/or insurance agent about factors that may suggest additional insurance coverage.

123

That's it.

In general, if you're in good health, and you want to replace your old life insurance, and it makes economic sense to do so, there would only be two reasons for you to NOT change your coverage:

1. You plan on committing suicide in the next two years.
2. You're going to lie when filling out your new application.

See, most life policies contain two provisions you should know about.

One is the "Suicide Clause." Simply stated, if you commit suicide within two years of getting a new policy, virtually all companies will not pay your claim. So, if suicide's not in your cards, this shouldn't affect you.

Secondly, there is the "Incontestability Period." This provision in most policies says that if you lie on your application, die in the first two years, and it's discovered that you lied on your application, the company does not have to pay a claim.

Other than health, there are only these two reasons to consider not replacing your coverage. (This assumes that your new policies will be a better value, that they'll be cheaper, or build a better savings amount or whatever, than your old policies.)

Anyway, we gave Fred and Carla two recommendations and a couple of options they could employ to take care of this insurance need.

We felt it was best for them to get the right amount of coverage based on the Capital Needs Analysis and to buy a single policy on each of their lives. Once the new policies were in place and in force, they were advised to cancel their old ones.

(Warning - Never cancel any existing policies until your new ones are paid for and in force. If your agent or planner suggests you do this, run to another advisor!)

We showed them one way to do this using Universal Life, with a second option of using term policies that would cover them for a number of years at a fixed premium, and no cash value savings.

We recommended both types of insurance have the exact face amount we established through the Needs Analysis. We then recommended two different types of policies with the correct amounts of coverage and had Fred and Carla choose which policy they were more comfortable with. As with any financial decision, there are always pros and cons.

They chose the Universal Life Policy because they felt the savings/investment features in the policy were something they wanted. They liked the forced savings idea more than paying for the life insurance with a term policy and not having any extra money going into the investment portion.

Now, their choice does not mean this is what you should do! Fred and Carla admitted they were lousy savers and liked the idea of combining the life coverage with a flexible savings plan. Many other clients like the idea of "buying term and investing the difference." That is, buy lower cost term life insurance and invest the money they would have paid into a cash value policy into something else.

Neither decision is, in and of itself, right or wrong. It depends on how you feel, what your circumstances are, and what you're most comfortable with. Which bring us to an interesting point.

See, as we said before, there's really only two kinds of life insurance. Although there are dozens and dozens of types within these two kinds, there are two and only two kinds. One is cash value insurance, and the second is term insurance.

Any cash value insurance policy, whether it's Universal, Whole life, Variable, whatever, has some sort of savings added to the premium you pay, so the money you pay goes into a savings account, which is tax-deferred, and you can borrow out (in some cases borrow it out without paying any income taxes). You are buying two things at once. You are buying the coverage you need, and you are building up a savings program.

We won't go into a long boring technical description of the different types of cash value insurance here, because there are so many, we'd be here all day. But we will give you a quick guide to the different categories, so you'll at least be armed with the right info when you talk to an advisor.

Whole Life: This is the most common type of cash value policy, since it was one of the first types of cash value policies. There are literally dozens of kinds of this type of policy and they all have minor differences. From your perspective, the most important feature to any Whole Life policy is that it has a fixed face amount, a fixed premium, and will earn some return on the cash value.

Some people still have old Whole Life policies that are badly out of date and incredibly expensive compared to modern policies. Many of these old Whole Life policies have an awful rate of return on the cash values. Chances are, if you own any Whole Life that's more than ten years old, you could replace it with a newer version of Whole Life or other cash value policy and end up with much better coverage.

WARNING!

Many companies HATE when you replace your old, expensive, out-of-date Whole Life policy with a modern policy that's more cost effective.

Why? Because they are making the biggest possible profit on those old policies.

Listen. Even though your agent, or planner, will have to fill out replacement forms when you switch policies, which will trigger a hysterical reaction from the old company, don't let any of this bother you!

If you agree with your planning assumptions and want to get the correct amount of insurance and like the new, higher value policy you're going to be switching to and you're not going to commit suicide or lie on the new application, YOURE ALLOWED TO IGNORE THE ATTACK FROM THE OLD COMPANY!

You don't have to talk to them. You don't have to respond to them. You don't have to do anything with them, or listen to them. (as long as you feel you are being provided with the correct, objective information you need and that switching policies is the right thing to do).

If you don't want to hassle with the old company or its salespeople, you can ask them to contact your new advisor, who will usually field the bombardment of letters and phone calls for you.

Another thing your old company might do is to tell you that you shouldn't switch. If that fails, they will often come back with a proposal of switching to one of their new policies that's just as good or "better" than the one you have applied for.

Isn't that interesting? Here they are, literally raking you over the coals for years, giving you a lousy product, and only now, when faced with replacement, they have a magical "better" policy for you.

Now, here's what we advise clients to ask them every time they do this:

"If you have had this new type of policy for the last seven years, why haven't you contacted me to switch to the obviously better value this new policy offers? Why did it take my working with a new advisor, who pointed out that your old policy was such a poor value, for you to magically "remember" that you have a better policy? Why didn't you contact me when this new policy became available? Would you have EVER contacted me to advise me of the better policy?"

Or something like that. OK?

To sum up, in general, older Whole Life policies are not very good values today. There are some newer Whole Life policies that are better than the older programs.

Enough on Whole Life. The bottom line is that no matter what the company says, you have to understand what you've got on your own or get help from an advisor.

Universal Life: This is a newer variety of life policy that came into effect in the last 20 years or so. Basically, it is similar to Whole Life, except that it offers more and usually higher growth on your savings.

For example, you can change the face amount and the premium without having to get a new policy like you would with most Whole Life products. So, if you wanted to lower your face value because something you were covering was no longer a factor in your life (e.g., paying off your mortgage) and you wanted to cut back on the life insurance costs, with Universal Life you could simply lower the face value, and correspondingly lower your premium. (Or, keep paying the same premium and build up more savings since you're paying for less coverage!)

There are differences between the guaranteed coverages and cash values offered with Universal Life versus Whole Life. You need to make sure you compare guarantees before making a decision. Also, whether you are looking at Whole Life or Universal Life, be sure the projections of coverage and cash value growth are realistic. For example, if interest rates on Treasury Bills are 5%, we would be suspicious of a projection that assumes interest rates will be averaging 12% in a life insurance policy for the next 20 years.

Like Whole Life, you can also access your cash value account if you want the money for some reason, usually in the form of a non-taxable loan. If you want a cash value policy and are willing to accept some risk of fluctuating interest rates, Universal Life is a good candidate in many cases.

Term Insurance: Term insurance, is basically where you just pay for the insurance. Like your auto or homeowners, it's a use-it-or-lose-it type approach.

They come in all flavors, but usually will lock in a premium schedule, which can be fixed or increasing, for a period of years.

It's pretty simple. When you die, the company pays your family (or whomever) the death benefit. If you cancel it before passing away, you get nothing. No cash value, no savings.

For some of you, this may be the best way to go. Just as long as you know your options and make an informed decision.

Which is better? The answer is, it depends. In some cases, you are better off buying the cash value policies because you like the idea of having some extra savings. Maybe you're not a good saver and you want to put the money away so you know it will be there.

The earnings on those policies are usually competitive, and sometimes guaranteed. Most companies are financially solvent and there is some additional protection for cash value insurance at the state level.

Other people who are real good savers and investors, and feel they can earn a whole lot more money on their savings and investments, might be better off "buying the term and investing the difference."

You're not going to hear this from too many people in the insurance business though. Most people in the insurance business are going to give you a definite opinion that one type is better than another, and that's just not true.

That's like saying everybody should have a manual transmission car, and someone else thinking everyone should have an automatic transmission car. There are advantages to both, and there are disadvantages to both. You have to decide on the input that's given to you (hopefully the facts) so you can make an educated decision.

We believe that people should know, first of all, how much they need, if any, and then decide if they want to buy some sort of a cash value product or some sort of a term product. That's it.

There are no other choices. If you really don't need any life insurance to take care of your spouse or your family when you pass away, but you would like to buy some insurance to leave an estate or to pay estate taxes or leave to a charity or whatever, that's fine. That's a personal decision you can make and fund with cash value insurance or term insurance.

We believe that you must understand how important it is to figure out how much insurance you need FIRST, and then SECOND, decide which kind of the two basic types of coverage you're going to use.

You must have education and information to make an objective, impartial, business-like decision about your life insurance. All the sales hype, all the hoopla, bells and whistles, songs and dances don't mean anything.

If the financial advisers you're working with aren't giving you an objective analysis of how much insurance you need, you shouldn't be working with them. And if they don't provide you with different types of policies to look at so you have options and can decide if you want to go with a cash value or term, or, in some cases - split the difference and buy some cash value coverage and some term coverage, getting the best in both worlds, you need to find new advisers.

Don't fall for sales pressure and hype.

We want to make it very clear that we are not anti-life insurance.

What we are against is life insurance being sold to you without first figuring how much you need, from an objective viewpoint, and your not having advice and information you need on the difference products that are available.

If the person you're working with tells you that you need so much insurance because you need x times your annual income, or you need enough to pay your debts, etc., that is not enough. You have to have a computer analysis to figure out inflation's effect on your income needs, taking into account your assets and liabilities, fixed income sources from pension and Social Security, and crunch all the numbers.

There is no other way to do it. No, it's not perfect. No, you will not get the exact answer, because it's impossible to come up with the exact answer. All that can be done is to give you the best possible answer using the most sensible assumptions. Then you have to decide if the assumptions make sense. Look at the different "what if" scenarios. Make sure you feel comfortable and then you can buy the insurance from an informed, planned approach. Anything short of this common sense, planning-based approach is not in your best interest.

One last word about life insurance that actually applies to any insurance plan we mention here. Some of these policies will not be available to everyone, in every state. Plus, what we write about today might change tomorrow, so please check and be careful before making decisions.

Another area of insurance very similar to life insurance with a great deal of confusion is... Long-Term Care Insurance.

Long-term care insurance covers a great need for most people. Fred and Carla, for example, had no long-term care insurance. When we asked them what would happen if either of them went into a nursing home in the near future and they had to spend an extra $3-5,000 a month to cover those costs (which is the national average), they were quite startled. The thought hadn't really occurred to them.

They had wrongly assumed that Medicare would pay for the costs, as most people do. So now that you know that Medicare pays for little, if anything, when it comes to nursing homes, and assuming you are not in the small number of people that will get the first 100 days paid for, what would you do if you had to come up with that kind of money every month?

In Fred and Carla's case, since they had a fairly decent amount of savings, but certainly not enough to cover those kinds of costs for a number of years if that was necessary, they would be wiped out in a year or so.

When we pointed this out to them and showed them the computer charts and graphs that clearly detailed what would happen to their estate if either of them were to go into a nursing home, and how fast they would run out of money, they became quite concerned. They agreed that long-term care insurance was necessary.

Now there aren't as many options available with long-term care insurance as there are with life insurance. Although there are a number of policies out there, most have basic features that cover a certain amount of time, a certain amount of money per day, with exclusions and limitations to what they will pay.

Whomever you are working with needs to show you one or two different types of polices so you can make a decision on which way to go.

Most policies require you to pay a monthly premium in exchange for them paying nursing home costs up to the limits of the policy if someone gets sick and goes into a nursing home.

At this time, many policies also pay benefits for home convalescent care. With the health-care situation we find ourselves in, it is very common now for people who don't really need skilled medical care to be at home, and because they are still confined, the policies will pay some or all of those costs.

The benefits and features of these policies vary widely. We could write a whole book about those features, exclusions, benefits, limitations, but we think the important information you need to know and need to ask is under what conditions will these policies pay, how much will they pay, are benefits increased with inflation, and how long are benefits paid for?

In Fred and Carla's case, since we were able to save them quite a bit of money each year on their life insurance by changing that around, we were able to take the money they used to pay on the life insurance and reposition it into paying for their long-term nursing care insurance.

Fred and Carla will end up with a slightly higher insurance cost than they used to pay, but now they will have both life insurance and long-term care insurance, instead of just life insurance!

Think about it.

The sole purpose of life insurance is to provide money for the family, or other interested entity like a business or charity, in the event of someone's death.

There are two main categories of policies:

Cash value policies:
- Whole Life
- Universal Life
- Variable Life

Term policies (No cash value).

In addition, you must look at Long-Term Care Insurance.

Auto and homeowners insurance should be set up so that you are basically covered for big disasters and not the small things. The small claims shouldn't be covered.

Consider a $2 million Liability Umbrella insurance policy.

Remember, the most important consideration is to have the right kind of insurance to protect you from big disasters.

Chapter 14

PUTTING IT ALL TOGETHER: GETTING YOUR PLAN STARTED TODAY

ℰℴ

We've covered a lot of material and a lot of information about taking care of yourself, financially-speaking, in retirement.

We've told you stories about lots of different kinds of people, what they've done right and what they've done wrong, and what we've done to help people have a peaceful and secure retirement.

You've gained a lot of information. Information that many people will not tell you and that some people would prefer you not have learned. You have discovered new ways of thinking, of doing things. You've had the truth revealed to you about the investment world, insurance, asset protection, Medicaid planning, etc.

You've learned a lot of things you won't learn other places, and you have an insight that most people will never get. You now have an advantage over the majority of Americans who haven't read the information contained in this book.

But all that information, knowledge and insight will be totally worthless if you don't start doing something about it and doing it right now. Everything we've taught you will go for naught if you don't take some action.

You must start implementing these strategies in order to change your situation.

A wise man once said,

"Motion is better than meditation."

Many people procrastinate even when they know they need to do something and take action, but they continue to think about it and delay the decision for some reason, or find excuses not to take action.

In fact, in our opinion, procrastination is the single biggest enemy of retirees.

It's the one action that is a total lack of action. Knowledge is worthless if it isn't used. Understanding and wisdom don't mean anything if they don't lead to results, and results won't happen if you don't take action.

The amazing thing is that no matter how many times we say this and how many times we repeat this message over and over, and try to motivate people into taking action, many people still won't do anything.

Maybe it's a fear of the unknown that paralyzes people like a deer staring at headlights in a road. Maybe they're confused, and as a result, don't want to take any action. Maybe they've listened to advice from other people, friends, relatives, and financial people that is so contradictory and confusing, they don't know what to do.

So they do nothing.

Maybe YOU'RE afraid of taking a portion of your money out of the bank. Maybe you've never used certain investments or savings accounts before, so they're all new. Maybe you've never really had investments. Maybe you've never really had a diversified portfolio. Maybe you've never seen all the investment options available to you.

Maybe, lots of things we've discussed are new to you, so you just leave what you already have, where it is.

As we've said before, the definition of insanity is doing the same things you've always done and expecting different results.

So, when you really think about it, if what you're doing right now isn't working, or if your intuition or instinct or actual results tell you it won't work...then you have to change what you're doing.

Doing the same things over and over and expecting new results is futile, hopeless and frustrating.

What does it take to get started? Sometimes the hardest thing for people to do is just get going a little bit. Once they get started, it's like a car at the top of a hill in neutral that gets a little push and begins moving forward, gaining momentum, speeding toward its destination.

We often find that if we can just get you to take one little action, and push you a little bit, you will start doing things. Once you start moving a little, and see how your plan and your financial life can change, you will take more actions and get on the path and move downhill yourself.

What does it take? In our opinion, it's not that difficult.

The single most important act for people to start <u>planning</u> is to actually <u>start</u> planning!

Yes, as basic as that sounds, we've discovered that if we can help people get into first gear and take some small actions like gathering all their financial papers together, they will get the rest of the planning going in short order.

So, all you have to do is get your stuff together.

That means going through the drawers or boxes, looking through your folders and finding out where you've put all your policies, statements, CD and bank information, investment accounts, wills, trusts, living trusts, pension information, accounts with your children, etc.

If you will gather all that, put it in a folder or shoe box or whatever, you'll be ready to meet with a financial professional who can start going through that information.

You will be amazed at how easily everything will go from there.

Many people we talk to take months and months to come into our office, just because they delayed putting their information together. We realize it's not the most fun job in the world. It's not the most exciting thing you can do, to look through drawers for your old tax returns, or looking for insurance policies you bought 30 years ago, or going to the safe deposit box and pulling out statements, policies, savings bonds, etc.

But, it may just be the single most important act you'll take! It'll start the ball rolling toward your goal of a well planned, carefully thought out financial life.

If you want a peaceful, secure retirement, PLANNING is the key!

But your advisors can't start the planning and you can't figure out what you're doing until you know everything you have. Once you've done that, you'll see the light at the end of the tunnel getting brighter and brighter.

Now this doesn't sound very complicated, and some people may read this and say, "Well, what's the big deal?" But, we can tell you from years and years of experience, this is a big deal - a very, very key point.

It's critical that you get started. Just getting started is half the battle. Once we get you started, you can begin your new life and your new plan today.

All it takes to get started is to just get started!

You will be relieved to get your planning going because the act of planning is very comforting and soothing. It's nice to take a look at what you're doing now and see just how you really are set up.

It feels good to see your situation as it is, and to start the actions to make sure you have the best chance of having a peaceful and secure retirement.

We have seen so many people breathe a sigh of relief when they finally took the step of beginning financial planning. We have seen the look of worry and doubt disappear as their plan unfolded. We have received hugs from people thanking us for helping them get their financial house in order.

Yes, it's a great feeling to start moving to a place you want to get to.

So just get started so you, too, can breathe that sigh of relief!

Think about it...

- **"Motion is better than meditation."**

- **The definition of insanity is "doing the same things you've always done before and expecting different results."**

- **The most single important act for people to start planning is to actually start planning.**

- **The best plan is worthless if it is not put into action!**

Chapter 15

HOW TO CHOOSE A TEAM OF ADVISORS
WHO WILL WORK FOR YOU!

&

WHY do you need a team of advisors and HOW do you find competent professionals to work with you?

No matter what you're doing -- designing a retirement plan, estate plan, tax plan, or investment plans -- you will need to hire the right people to help you achieve your goals. Your responsibility is to determine and map out your goals, and then let a competent professional team help you get what you want!

First, you have to realize that everyone needs help at one time or another. It's just a fact of life. The world is so complex, and nobody, repeat nobody, knows everything. Not you, or anybody else knows everything.

That's why when you have an operation, there's a surgeon, an anesthesiologist, scrub nurses, nursing technicians, and a host of other highly trained individuals. That's because they know a team of people who are specialists in certain areas will make the procedure go like clock-work.

They depend on each other, and you depend on them. They couldn't perform the surgery alone, just as none one of us could perform surgery on ourselves.

So why, when it comes to financial matters, do most people think they can pick up an investment magazine and become their own financial advisor overnight?

How can someone, who hasn't intensely studied this specialized field, believe they can know it all and handle it all by themselves just from a magazine? Or from a friend or neighbor's advice?

Who should you have on your team?

Although every situation is different, most individuals need a group of competent professionals to work together in achieving optimum results for you.

In general, you should build a team of advisors who can work together and strive to achieve the same goal... YOUR GOALS! But so many people become fearful or neglectful of putting together their own team of people who can stabilize and secure their current and future financial well-being.

- **Many don't understand the complexity of finance and taxes.**

136

- **Many are afraid to seek help, because they don't know what to ask.**
- **Many don't know how to find a good team of advisors.**
- **Many don't know what duties to give to each team member!**

It is difficult, we'll agree. But in general, most individuals who are concerned about a peaceful and secure retirement should, at a minimum, work with: a financial advisor, an accountant, an estate planning attorney, and/or an investment counselor.

The biggest thing to remember is not to cut corners. Don't think that your attorney can give you great investment advice, or that your insurance agent can best decide how to structure your deductions for tax purposes.

Most of all, the professional who claims to know it all probably knows very little!

Who Should Be In Charge?

Other than you making the ultimate decisions, once you've been given all your options to weigh, you'll typically need someone to run the show. Depending on how you approach planning, and whom you've worked with the longest, one of your advisors will most likely serve in the leadership role.

This leader should help you coordinate the tasks and responsibilities of each advisor.

This leader will be the quarterback just like in football. Your financial quarterback should walk you through the process. This leader will be different for each individual. It may be your accountant, the estate planning attorney, or the financial advisor. It doesn't really matter, as long as they have "what it takes" to take charge.

And when we say ``take charge'', we mean the one who makes sure things are done according to YOUR wishes.

It does NOT mean the financial advisor tells the attorney how to draft documents or tells the investment planner which investment to pick. Each advisor needs to carry his or her own weight and be allowed to do the job they were trained to do.

And the end result should always be to get YOU to where YOU want to be!

How should the team of advisors work together?

Well, first and foremost, all of your advisors need to talk to each other. This sounds so simple, but it so rarely happens! And many times it's not the fault of the professional. Most people go to an accountant for one thing, see their attorney for another, and get investment advice from someone else, without seeing how one will affect the other.

137

The fact is that they absolutely affect each other, and it's critical that each of your planning elements be tied together.

Think about it. When was the last time your attorney, accountant, financial advisor and insurance agent all sat down together, or conversed over the phone, to make sure that they were working in harmony to achieve your goals?

The answer to this question is typically, "Never!"

What happens if they don't get along?

If you're advisors don't work well together because of their egos or personalities, replace one, part, or all of the team. Keep in mind, they work for YOU!

There are two significant problems people face when putting their team together:

1. The client thinks that only one advisor is enough. They think this advisor knows about all areas of the tax law, investments, insurance, etc. From what you've read, you know this is not the case.

2. Many advisors are quick to say "no," and take the safe road of inaction, rather than help the client achieve their goals. They don't want to risk being held liable for giving some wrong advice.

Well, how would you feel if you went to the doctor, and instead of hearing about all the new and alternative treatments for cancer, the doctor kept his mouth shut? Or, if the doctor heard of a new pill you could take to kill the cancer, but didn't tell you? It's your life and you should decide what risks you'll take.

If your team of advisors does not have an open mind to new planning techniques, it may be as bad as the doctor example. They need to constantly keep up with the times and keep you well aware of any changes, strategies, and alternative options.

If your advisors don't stay up with the changes in their fields, how can they properly advise you? And, that's what you've hired and paid them to do, isn't it?

In fact, it would be a good idea to get some references from them. See if they're willing to share any, and ask those folks how pleased they were with that particular person. It's just like an interview -- get to the heart of this person, check them out thoroughly, check references, and then continuously monitor their work. If they excel, you keep them. If they're lazy or inept, you fire them.

Who really is the client? You are, of course! And, you are doing them a favor by hiring them. NOT THE OTHER WAY AROUND! They work for you, not the other way around.

There should always be a mutual respect for all parties. Your advisors should serve you, but not be your servants. They should be able to advise you without you forcing them into it, or without them forcing you to do something that you don't want to do or don't understand.

And don't let them intimidate you. Some will, on purpose, to show off their knowledge. Most don't. Some people perceive knowledge as intimidating, because they are the intimidated by their own lack of knowledge and understanding.

To sum things up, various people are needed to help you achieve your goals. You need every element of your planning to be backed by competent individuals. And all of these individuals need to be up to speed in their specialized fields and keep you informed along the way. Although they have different and very distinct responsibilities, they all need to work closely together for you.

Like a good military operation, surgery or team sport, no one can do it all on their own, and everyone must understand your goals and work together to achieve them!

Think about it ...

- **You will need to hire the right people to help you achieve your goals. Your responsibility is to determine and map out your goals, and then let a competent professional team help get you what you want.**

- **You need to build a team of advisors who can work together and strive to achieve the same goal... YOUR GOALS.**

- **Remember, YOU are the client, NOT THEM! They work for you, not the other way around.**

- **Other than you making the ultimate decisions, once you've been given all your options to weigh, you'll need someone to run the show. Depending on how you approach planning, and whom you've worked with the longest, one of your advisors will most likely serve in the leadership role.**

- **There should be only one lead advisor**

In conclusion, after talking about planning throughout this whole book, we are now reminding you that the best way, the only way, to make sure your finances are on track, is to start planning right now.

If you want to know if you're OK, if you want to know if you're doing things right for your situation, if you want to know what choices you have so you can make educated decisions, you must begin to plan right away!

As the slogan from Nike goes, "Just Do It"!